It's a Guy Thing

IT'S A GUY THING

An Owner's Manual *for* Women

DAVID DEIDA

Health Communications, Inc.
Deerfield Beach, Florida
www.hcibooks.com

Library of Congress Cataloging-in-Publication Data

Deida, David.
    It's a guy thing : an owner's manual for women / David Deida.
        p.   cm.
    ISBN-13: 978-1-55874-464-6 (trade paperback)
    ISBN-10: 1-55874-464-9 (trade paperback)
        1. Man-woman relationships—United States. 2. Men—United
    States—Psychology. 3. Women—United States—Psychology.
    4. Intimacy (Psychology)—United States. 5. Interpersonal com-
    munication—United States.   I. Title.
    HQ801.D44974 1997
    306.7—dc21   97-21703
                                                                         CIP

HCI, its logos and marks are trademarks of
Health Communications, Inc.

Publisher: Health Communications, Inc.
                    3201 S.W. 15th Street
                    Deerfield Beach, Florida 33442-8190

Cover design by Lawna Patterson Oldfield

CONTENTS

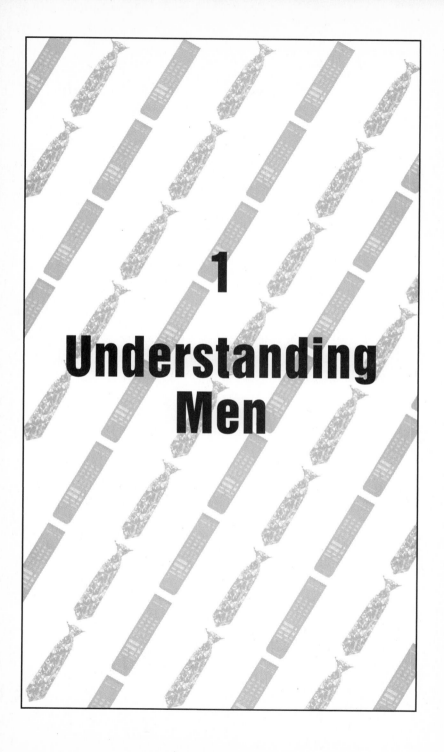

1
Understanding
Men

Why Are Men So Difficult?

Most women, at one time or another, have wondered why their man was so difficult—why, on occasion, he behaved like a jerk. The answer is easy: Most men "give out" masculine energy. This, at times, is offensive to most women. What do I mean by "masculine energy"?

Every man and woman has both masculine and feminine energy within them. In about 10 percent of all men, these energies balance. Another 10 percent of all men demonstrate more feminine energy than masculine. But about 80 percent of all men demonstrate more masculine than feminine energy. These men can often seem like jerks.

These men are difficult for most women to deal with in intimacy because masculine energy is very different from feminine energy—and about 80 percent of women are naturally more feminine than masculine. Intimate relationships between a masculine man and a feminine woman often seem like a struggle between creatures from different planets. They try to communicate with one another in a language neither understands.

Many men seem like jerks to many women because feminine energy is frequently confused, offended and hurt by the masculine, just as the masculine is by feminine energy. Once understood, the differences between masculine and feminine can become gifts men and women offer to one another in passionate love, rather than wrinkles to be ironed out.

Why Is He So Rigid?

One masculine quality is modality, the ability to focus. Masculine energy tends to focus on doing one thing at a time. It moves on a single track. Have you ever tried to interrupt a man while he is absorbed in a project? Many men just won't notice you or else they will become angry and resentful.

The feminine is much less modal. It's not stuck on a single track. It flows easily from one thing to another. It's much easier for a man or woman using their feminine energy to do several things at once. When men use their masculine energy, they may feel everything is falling apart when they are called on to do more than one thing at a time, or when they are suddenly pulled off a project.

Why Doesn't He Pay More Attention to Me?

In both sexes, masculine energy is a vehicle of focus and accomplishment. This energy eliminates distraction and focuses on what needs to be done.

For instance, when most men watch TV or work on a project, the rest of the world ceases to exist. That includes their intimate relationship. Even if the project is as mundane as waxing a car, masculine energy will focus and shut out the rest of the world.

Masculine energy has the ability to focus. It's a strength, but a strength that can turn to weakness when it's used to avoid an intimate relationship.

Feminine energy is quite good at flowing and relaxing. If your feminine energy is at work while waxing the car and your partner wants to talk with you, you can easily shift your attention and focus.

Men often find it very difficult to shift, because they are stuck in their masculine energy. It's not easy for most men to break what they are doing, shift their attention to you and then flow back again. For women who are comfortable with their feminine energy, this ability to shift happens almost automatically.

Many women might feel, *Why isn't he paying attention to me?*, *What's his problem?* You could take it personally, believing he's choosing to neglect you.

If a woman friend were to neglect you it would send a definite message. Most women are very aware of relationships. But for men, absorption into a project or TV is rarely designed to send a message. It's just how they do things. That's how masculine energy works.

Women often ask, "Can't my man learn to go with the flow? Can't he be more flexible? Why does he have to be so rigid and single-minded?"

Men may wonder, "Why does she get hurt when I'm busy? Can't she understand it's not personal? What a hassle! She gets hurt every time I'm doing what I like to do. Can't she change?"

If you want to trust your man to get the job done, try to accept his need to focus. Without this quality, your man might not carry through with projects he starts. You would begin to feel like you had to do them yourself. You would lose trust in him.

You can't expect a man to get things done and not be focused. For a man to drop this quality he has to move into his feminine energy, where he may lose his focus and fail to get the job done.

Why Does His Work Seem More Important Than Me?

When your man is hard at work, it doesn't necessarily mean he's shutting you out. He's not being insensitive, turning away or avoiding participation with you. When he's focused on a project or a task, that becomes the whole world to him.

Men are either in one mode or another. For instance, a man could be having problems with his wife yet still enjoy an outing with his male friends. On a fishing trip a friend could ask, "How are things at home?" He'll say, "Man, it sucks. Wow, look at the size of that fish!"

For most women, or anyone in their feminine energy, the intimate relationship touches their lives no matter what they're doing. It's difficult to drop the relationship, get absorbed in something, enjoy it completely, then go back to the relationship.

A man who temporarily "forgets" his relationship may not be avoiding his feelings. The same thing may happen to you when you are in your masculine energy. When the masculine energy focuses, everything else disappears.

If you were in the midst of an emotionally charged thought or feeling and your partner said "Can you get the catsup for me?", it would disrupt your emotions and probably frustrate you. When you inject your emotional mode into his action mode, it feels the same way to him.

Men don't exist so much in a world of flow and feelings. To a large extent, they exist in a world of problems, functions and challenges.

Most archetypal myths of men involve battling demons, enemies, war and conquest. They involve breaking free and winning. Most archetypal myths about women involve love relationships. Men and women play in very different domains. If you want to be married to a masculine man, as opposed to a feminine or more neutral man, then part of the package you get is his modality, his ability to focus.

When your man thinks your emotions are wrong, it can throw off the whole relationship. Emotions can't be *wrong*, they simply *are*. In the same way, his action mode is not wrong, it just is. But this doesn't mean you can't gift him with your feelings, sensitivity, intuition and wisdom.

Two of the biggest gifts you bring to your man are your sensitivity and intuition. He can learn a lot from your world that is foreign to his. And you can also learn from him.

Don't disown your feelings. If you really feel it's best for him to be interrupted, then interrupt him. Just remember that you may encounter some initial resentment, because he's stuck in one mode.

Why Isn't He Aware of How He Hurts Me?

When your man gets involved in something and doesn't pay attention to you, it hurts. He probably doesn't feel he's turning away from you. He may not be aware of it at all.

When your man turns away or becomes involved in something else, you could say, "Did you notice that half an hour ago we were making love when the phone rang? Since you hung up you haven't even looked at me." He'll look puzzled, and mumble "Yeah, okay."

You could also say, "I felt a sudden shift in your attention. One moment we were passionate, the next moment nothing. Our hearts were connected, and now they are not." It will seem bizarre to you that he doesn't feel any of this, but he usually doesn't.

When I lead men's groups, we spend a lot of time talking about this. I try to convince the men that women do feel the shifts in a man's attention. The men don't believe it. They'll say, "You're kidding, right?" I'll say, "I'm serious. If you're with a woman and you suddenly turn away and begin to work, she feels it in her body. She feels your attention moving away from her. She feels hurt." The men will usually respond, "How are you supposed to live with that?"

Men often have no idea they've hurt you. When you tell them, it helps if you understand their perspective. Talk to them as if they've fallen asleep and reawakened. So rather than criticize their actions, tell them how it makes you feel. Say, "When you picked up the phone I felt hurt," rather than "Don't pick up the phone when we are together." You can tell them how it makes you feel. Then they can handle it.

But if you expect a man to know they've hurt you, they'll say, "What hurt you?" They don't sense the turning away is as hurtful as it is to you.

What Can I Do When He Seems So Burdened?

At their core, most men feel constrained by life. It is a struggle for men to simply enjoy life. Most everything feels like a constraint and an obligation to them. It sometimes feels this way to women also, but for most men it always feels this way.

Have you seen the bumper stickers that say, "Life sucks"? That's the masculine motto. That's why all men are driven either to escape or conquer life. They may do this by becoming absorbed in the newspaper, watching TV, making a lot of money, using drugs, or even by practicing meditations which promise to help them transcend daily life.

Daily life. Being in a body, having relationships, caring for children, needing to eat. Existence seems like a burden or a challenge to most men, something to work on or escape from, something to conquer.

Because a woman is so connected to life, it's hard for her to understand the need to conquer or escape it. But for most men, even being in a body is a problem. If a man is the conqueror type, he will attempt to push his body and make it do what he wants, applying his energy to push toward victory in the affairs of life.

For a man life seems like a constraint, be it his body, his relationship or his work—until he learns to practice love. Just like Jesus on the cross, most men feel crucified by life. A spiritually mature man learns to love in the midst of this crucifixion. Even so, he may still feel like life is a sacrifice.

I'm overstating this to make a point, but men are always attempting to do something with life, because they are not at home in life. Rarely is a man capable of being love in the midst of life, submitting to the crucifixion, suffering life's limitations, and yet bringing love into his relationships.

Some of your special gifts to your man as his chosen woman are energy and attraction. You attract him toward life by your radiance, and give him the energy to endure the crucifixions of life through the power of your love.

Your gifts of energy, of radiance, of attraction, may take the form of your genuine smile, the look of love in your eyes, your touch that enlivens him, anything that fills his body, mind and emotions with energy, love and life. Then he feels you as his source of delight in an otherwise burdensome world.

Why Is He So Obsessed with Perfection?

Men, or anyone in their masculine energy, typically seek perfection. It could be the perfect wax job on the car, or the perfect wave to surf, or the perfect touchdown. Women, of course, also seek perfection at times. But the feminine priority, in man or woman, is usually the desire for love.

If you, as a woman, are suffering in a poor relationship, how much will you enjoy the "perfect" wax job on your car? Many men, however, become totally obsessed with things like that even in the midst of a painful relationship. In fact, they *particularly* become obsessed by things like that during painful times. It's their little way of engaging in the perfection of unblemished consciousness, consciousness that is always perfect.

Our masculine and feminine ways are not only rooted in our biological roots, but also in our spiritual depths. As it has been said in many spiritual traditions, the first thing created was light. This light is the true source of our feminine energy, and the void in which it shines is the source of our masculine.

That's why many women are concerned with their radiance. They identify themselves as sources of light or energy. They want shiny hair, glossy lips, blushed cheeks, glowing skin, radiant eyes. The feminine in each of us feels akin to life force itself.

The masculine in each of us feels more akin to the void in which the light shines. Most men would rather watch women dance than dance themselves. They want to witness feminine radiance. Thus, men identify more with the witness, with awareness, with consciousness itself.

This consciousness never moves, while the feminine energy always moves. This consciousness never changes, while the feminine energy always changes. Men who stand firm and trustable in their deep truth are more sexy to women. Women who move their bodies freely in radiant energy are more sexy to men.

Men seek perfection in the external world—in their philosophies, golf games and a centerfold's body—because they intuit the perfection of deep and eternal consciousness. But they misplace this desire for perfection. Deep consciousness, or divine consciousness, may be perfect, changeless and unblemished, but life is not. Life is the play of energy. Life is feminine!

Anything that is alive is not perfect, though men try to make it so. They try to perfect their golf game. They fantasize over perfect women's bodies. They try to understand the perfect philosophy. Men seek perfection because they intuit the nature of consciousness, which is unchanging.

Changeless perfection is irrelevant for the feminine. The feminine is interested in love and life, and life includes birth and death and change. Life is not unchanging and perfect all the time.

For consciousness purists, however, change is anathema. Men, especially when feeling threatened by the feminine, want to retreat from the changes of life into perfection, voidness, or unchanging abstraction.

They become immersed in a newspaper, or in TV, something that removes them from the problems of life. Or, they become focused obsessively on perfection in some trivial form, because that's the closest they can get to the perfection of unblemished consciousness. Men are most at home in projects, sports, philosophy and ideas outside of the daily ups and downs of life.

If a woman is obsessed with perfection, she has probably rejected her own feminine. For some reason, she has identified with her masculine energy. Just as men must learn to embrace life and love in order to become whole, perfectionist women must learn to embrace the feminine part of themselves and others. This begins with an embrace of the body itself: a sensuous appreciation for the body, for bodily pleasure, for the body's wild energy, for the body's beauty, for a full, sweet breath, and a soft, open heart. This embrace of the feminine is also the cure for a man's obsessive perfectionism. If men don't embrace the fullness of life, of feminine change, then they become one-sided. Men need to learn that if they want light, radiance and energy in their life then they need to embrace all the changes and so-called "blemishes," too.

Why Do I Feel Him Rejecting Me So Often?

The primary masculine fear is the fear of failure in life. The primary feminine fear is the fear of rejection in a relationship, the fear of the loss of love. These fears motivate you and your man differently.

It's a masculine obsession; men love to solve problems. If there is a problem, all your man's energy will go into solving it. If you, as a woman, are also in your masculine energy, you will be aligned to solving problems, too. But in your feminine energy, you'll feel him turn his attention away from you toward the problem.

Imagine that your man gets a call from the bank telling him his account is overdrawn. For him, this becomes an immediate priority. His whole mind and body abruptly turn toward the problem and away from you. Even if you were making love the moment before he got the phone call, suddenly he has a problem that needs to be solved. You will feel his attention swiftly moving away from you. You may react by withdrawing from him, assuming that he is consciously turning away from you.

But these responses are simply the feminine and masculine energies at work. You are in your feminine and are sensitive to the relationship. You're afraid of losing his love. He is sensitive to the problems that have to be solved in his life. He's in his masculine mode of analysis and action. He's afraid of failure.

He's not acting the way he does to send you a message. He's acting this way because it's the way his masculine energy moves.

You're not responding the way you are in order to hurt him. Yet the fact remains, you both feel hurt.

You may feel his attention to problem solving is a rejection of you, a betrayal of you. If this causes you to pull back from him, he will feel your withdrawal as rejection. He might think: "Here I am, taking care of my life, and she's pulling away." He doesn't know you feel hurt and rejected. He's unaware of your inner feelings. But he is aware of whether you are supporting him or withdrawing from him.

The masculine energy looks to the feminine energy for life-giving, radiance-giving, love-giving support. He needs your support most when he gets into his world of problem solving. If you feel rejected and you close down or withdraw, he will feel your withdrawal of energy as a rejection of him, just like you felt his withdrawal of energy from you.

You are withholding because his attention went elsewhere. He may then withhold because he feels unsupported. Suddenly, you each feel the other withdrawing. Suddenly, there is a tension between you. You both feel unloved and unsupported.

When your man turns away from you to solve a problem, realize that is his need. It may even be his way of supporting you and serving you. Notice if you are responding to his absorption in problem solving by withdrawing yourself, feeling rejected or angry. All too often he is not consciously turning away from you at all; he may even feel that solving a problem is one of the ways he cares for you.

Your man should learn to communicate his needs to you in a loving way. He should learn to take your heart connection into account, so that his need to solve problems doesn't violate your need for love. But in the meantime, understanding his fear of failure will help you deal with his abruptness.

Why Can't He Be with Me Emotionally?

Emotionality is not the same as love. Masculine love is often silent, discriminative, penetrating or unwavering. Feminine love is often tearful, excited, wild or joyous. Love is love; it can be expressed in many forms.

Many women experience strong emotions from day to day, often triggered by other people's love or rejection of them.

They often assume that men must experience these same emotions. Some men do, but others don't. Just as men must stop demanding that women always analyze their feelings, women must stop demanding that men always express themselves through emotionality.

The true obligation in relationship for both men and women is to transcend the changing flow of emotions and thoughts and directly give love. This is the key to the daily practice of intimacy. *No matter what you are feeling or thinking, practice giving and receiving love.* Feminine emotionality and masculine analysis are merely two styles of communication. One is not more loving than the other.

Whether you are willing to open and love is more important than the style by which you express yourself. Instead of obliging your partner to be more emotional, locate your true heart. Breathe from your true heart. Locate your true heart, the depth of your authentic being. Relax into your true heart. In your true heart there is no reactivity, no withdrawal, no need to punish others when they are not loving. Your true heart—the deepest core of your being—may be wounded, but even so, it still wants to give and receive love. Through the beauty of your open heart, your man may learn to relax more into his true heart, whether his style of loving is more emotional or not.

Why Is He Afraid to Commit?

The quest for freedom is most important to the masculine energy. That freedom can be financial, professional, artistic or spiritual. The most important priority for the feminine

energy is relationship and love. When your man turns away
from you, you may instantly feel, "I must be doing something
wrong. I must be doing something wrong or he would want
to spend more time with me."

Most men, if forced to make a choice between an intimate
relationship or their art/profession/spiritual path, will choose
the latter. When a woman is in her masculine energy she will
make the same choice: freedom over love.

If you are in your feminine, love and an intimate relationship
is at the core of your life. But at the core of your man's life is
his quest for freedom from constraints. He will do anything to
continue on his quest. If he imagines your relationship is going
to limit his quest, he will not want to commit. He'll want to
keep things open.

When men enter more deeply into a relationship, they feel
their attention being more absorbed in love for you. This may
scare them. They imagine that their freedom is decreasing,
and they react by pulling out, or by refusing to make a commitment to the relationship, especially following an increased
period of depth of intimacy.

Why Can't He Be More Vulnerable?

You may feel that your man is not vulnerable. You may
feel that he has built walls around himself. Indeed, he may
not want you, or anyone else, to enter into his life. He may be
very rigid and invulnerable. But there may also be something
else happening.

It is possible that what you call vulnerability is the feminine form of vulnerability. Masculine vulnerability is quite

different. When a man is vulnerable he may not talk about his feelings as much. When a man is vulnerable, he usually talks about his vision, or his lack of it.

The most vulnerable place of a man's life often has very little to do with the same emotions that are central to a woman's life. A man's vulnerability has more to do with considerations such as, "Am I living my life fully?" "Am I following my highest vision?" "Am I going in the right direction?" "Am I wasting my life?"

"I'm feeling bad in this relationship," is rarely a central issue for a man. He may question his relationship, but more as a part of the overall scheme of his life rather than its central issue. A man's most vulnerable place has to do with his direction in life. When he feels vulnerable, he may question whether he is living his truth.

Sometimes your man is truly not open to you. But perhaps what you call "open" is different for you and your man. Entertain the possibility that when he speaks of his direction in life he is being most vulnerable. If you do, then you'll appreciate his openness as a man. When men talk about their direction in life, they are opening some of the most central parts of themselves to you.

2

Thank God Women Are Not Men

Can Geographical Places Have Sexual Characteristics?

The Hawaiian island of Kauai is very feminine. If you take a walk on Kauai, no matter what you were previously doing, your whole body breathes fully and feels full of joy. There are double rainbows, beautiful bird songs and the fragrance of tropical fruit and beautiful flowers all around you. The surrounding ocean is healing and rejuvenating. Some of Kauai's feminine qualities are its healing properties, its radiance, its fertility, and the feeling that life is abundant.

Life itself is feminine. Anything that has to do with life is feminine. The forces of nature are feminine. Even in our secular culture, we recognize nature to be feminine. And before it became politically correct to do otherwise, all hurricanes and typhoons were named after women.

The feminine has another side to it, too, as does Kauai. Kauai has monsoon-like rains, hurricanes and rip tides, as well as rainbows and flowers. These chaotic, wild qualities are also part of the feminine, just as much as the healing and life-giving qualities are.

New York, on the other hand, is a very masculine city. It is full of focused energy. Most people there are on a mission of some kind. They are intensely directed. Some of the masculine qualities are one-pointedness, goal-orientation and purposeful focus. The masculine eliminates obstructions to pursue and reach a goal. On the streets of New York, for instance, you walk with a purpose. You stay focused and don't act too friendly with strangers. This narrow, directional quality is a masculine quality, whether it is in a man or a woman or a city.

In New York, everything moves upward. Skyscrapers go

up, elevators go up, and people go up the success ladder as well as up into their heads. The masculine quality points up and ahead. Men, or anyone in their masculine energy, tend to be in their heads more than their bodies.

In Hawaii, though, men and women can relax into their feminine and their bodies. They relax in the healing ocean. They play on the warm, soft sand. They smile at strangers and greet one another with a friendly, "Aloha."

The masculine and feminine are universal energies. You find them not only in men and women, but also in places, animals and even objects. By understanding the universal energies of masculine and feminine, we can smile rather than argue about differences between ourselves and our intimate partners.

Why Do Men and Women Shop So Differently?

There is a real difference between the way men and women shop. Men usually know what they want, go into the store and get it.

Most women, rather than darting in and out, search through a store and check things out. If you are in your masculine, your partner's feminine and flowing way of shopping drives you crazy. If you are in your feminine, this way of shopping is very enjoyable.

Why Do We Fight So Much?

Often, arguments arise because women want their partners to be more like them. Women typically want men to make more of a commitment to the relationship and to express their feelings about the intimacy. Women want men to pay more attention and spend more time with them in an intimate, romantic and loving way. That is, women want men to be more like women.

Men want women to be more sexually available, less moody and less talkative about their feelings and the details of their day. Men want women to "keep their word" and talk straight about what they want to do. That is, men want women to be more like men.

This desire to want your partner to be more like you results in conflicts. Unless you understand, honor and appreciate the differences in one another, you will be in conflict. It is inevitable because you, as a woman, will always crave more intimacy and communication. He will always crave your ability to get to the point and be less moody. Rather than compete, you can complement one another with your sexual differences. Then, when you fight, you won't try to prove you're right, but will enjoy the play of differences. In fact, in Chinese, the symbol for sex translates to "flowery combat."

What Are the Essences of Masculine and Feminine?

Masculine strength is confidence of your direction in life. In order for a woman to trust a man fully, she must feel his self-confidence and direction. One reason men and women should clarify their masculine energy is so they have a clear vision of their lives and where they want them to go.

If your man is always wishy-washy and never knows what he wants to do, it is difficult to trust him as a life partner. A good partner is a man who is strong in his vision and direction. He also embraces you. He appreciates and honors you not only as a person but as a unique woman, as his cherished connection to the feminine aspect of the universe.

The feminine qualities include the ability to give love, nurturing and bring radiance to life, which attracts people into their bodies and their hearts. The more a woman does this, the more attractive she is to her man. Men are always attracted to radiant women. Radiance does not depend on specific physical features. Radiance is the beauty which shines from a woman's happiness. It is the shine of her love.

Through nonjudgmental observation, we can discover how we limit our masculine strength of vision and our feminine strength of radiance. By venturing beyond our fears, doubts and uncertainties, men and women continue to grow sexually, emotionally and spiritually.

What Do Soap Operas and Sex Movies Have in Common?

Soap operas and romance novels are women's pornography. Women disconnect from love when they lose themselves in the drama of emotions, just as men disconnect from love when they lose themselves in genital stimulation.

Many men complain about how difficult it is to communicate with a woman lost in her emotions. Many women complain that their man is too mechanical during sex. Neither soap operas nor sex movies are about love; they are about emotional dramatization and genital stimulation.

Men complain that women don't communicate very clearly. A man asks his partner, "What are you feeling?" and she can't answer in three words or less. Men constantly complain that women can't focus clearly because they are so emotionally dramatic.

Men want their women to be more like men; men mean what they say; their word is final. When a man shakes hands on something that's that. It doesn't matter if his emotions change. He carries through with the agreement—or knows that he has failed.

Men become frustrated when a woman is too emotional to communicate her intentions clearly, or when she changes her mind: "This is impossible! I want a woman I can communicate with! She drives me crazy! Why do they always say they will do one thing, then do something else!" He gets very frustrated. Meanwhile, she withdraws more and eventually closes down.

A woman wants to feel a connection with her partner. She wants him to understand and validate her emotions. She wants to be felt. She wants to be loved. She wants him to be sensitive to her feelings rather than be so rigid about what she said she would do.

Both men and women demand the other be more like themselves. The message is, "Unless you are more like me, I can't love you. Unless you stick to your word (or are sensitive to my feelings), I get angry (or hurt)."

A man tends to be in his mind and focused. A woman tends to be in her emotions. In order to give love to one another they must meet in the common ground of the heart: love.

Perhaps it would be good for men to become as emotionally expressive as women. Perhaps it would be good for women to say what they mean and not change their minds. This would make relationships easier, but it's unlikely to happen very soon. In the meantime, men and women could practice giving and receiving love without trying to make their partner more like themselves.

Why Does He Say I'm Too Emotional When He Seems So Rigid?

This question points to a very common source of conflict in relationships.

For example, you might make a beautiful meal for your man. You sit down to eat together and he seems very grateful. He feels loved by you. Then, out of the corner of his eye he sees a magazine. He picks it up, starts reading, and suddenly he's totally focused on reading. You'll be hurt by this if you interpret his actions in terms that don't apply to men.

Instead, you must realize that he is probably not consciously turning away from you. He has become absorbed in a mode which is a liability of the masculine. He can't help it. Your gift to him is to invite him out of his mode back into relationship with you, back into love.

Men who don't get invited out of their focus become fascist, rigid and one-dimensional. Men who aren't gifted with femininity become obsessively driven toward a goal. World destructive politics are based on this masculine dissociation.

On the other hand, when the feminine is not balanced by the masculine, it becomes addictive. Without masculine

self-discipline and direction, you become addicted to chocolate, coffee, relationships, all kinds of things. If you don't have
the masculine edge brought into your life, there is a tendency
to flow along, losing yourself in whatever you are involved
with. Excessive masculine energy leads to abuse of others and
the world; excessive feminine energy leads to self abuse.

To men, I often suggest that they learn to enjoy a woman's
emotional fullness and embrace her in love regardless of her
mood. The men say, "Embrace her emotions? She seems
crazy!"

To women, I often suggest they treat their man as a weary
warrior. I suggest that women learn to enjoy their man's
focus and direction because that's how men are. But invite
them out. Attract them into love. Fill their weary hearts with
your energy. Your loving energy will loosen his rigid stance.
His embrace will penetrate your emotions with love.

Why Can't He Love Me
When His Career Isn't Going Well?

It is usually easier for a woman to love her man when her
job isn't going well than it is for a man to love his woman
when his job isn't working out. When your man is fully loving you, you can share love with him even though your career
isn't going well. You are capable of sharing love with your
partner even while you work out the problems in your career
because love is your priority.

But your man may not be fully capable of sharing love
while his career isn't going well since his quest for direction
and freedom is most likely his priority. A woman might say

to her man, "Why can't you love me? I love you. Can't you be with me even though your project isn't going well?" But he can't be with her fully until he has aligned his life with his vision and begins to take care of business.

For the feminine, love is the priority. Since the feminine has the ability to shift energy, it is possible for you to love and still take care of other projects.

Within each man and woman, the masculine energy puts work before intimacy, whereas the feminine energy puts intimacy before work. Which part of yourself you choose to follow is up to you. Neither is wrong, and both masculine and feminine are worthy of respect, in both you and your partner.

Why Does He Like to Go Places Without Me?

Traditionally, most women have found their unique way of life in community, sharing with other women. The feminine connects with the flow of life. So, if the culture is healthy, women are naturally connected with who they are. They intuitively feel their place in the whole of the living world.

The masculine, however, disconnects from life to find its purpose. The masculine always tries to figure out a way to integrate into life. Men must find their purpose and bring it back home. It's not something they find in the natural flow of life, or in their intimate relationships.

Most women, in a healthy culture, are already in the flow of love, already connected with what they love doing. Of course, very few cultures are healthy now, so most women, like most men, have lost connection with their essence. Women traditionally have opened to the earth, to all of nature, to the birth of new life, and to life with others, in order to rediscover their essence.

Most women find their purpose *inside* of life and intimate relationship. Most men find their purpose *outside* of life and intimate relationship. For instance, American Indian men might dance in the sun for days, or go on a vision quest without food or water, to reconnect with their purpose. This isn't exactly everyday life.

Most men go outside of life to experience their purpose. They leave their relationships behind, temporarily. Their struggle is to bring their discovered vision back into their life, and back into their intimate relationship. Women find their essential purpose in life, as a lover of life. Their idea of filling their body and heart with love rarely involves going out into no-man's land, hoping to receive a vision before dying of exposure.

Men find their essence by way of the quest. For women, it is a matter of magnifying love in a relationship. The archetype for men is the search for the Holy Grail, risking their lives, surviving, discovering and returning. The archetype for women is falling in love, discovering the ways of love and giving love. Women struggle to love, overcoming their doubt of love and their resistance to love. For men it is a struggle of, "Why the hell exist? I have to find out."

We each have masculine and feminine energy within ourselves. So each of us, man and woman alike, must find our ultimate purpose and overcome our doubt of love.

3

The Snap, Crackle and Pop of Sex

What Is Sexual Polarity?

How do we maintain love and passion in our intimate relationships for more than a few months? How do we regenerate love and desire for one another year after year?

Relationships are great at the beginning. Almost all new relationships are incredibly exciting and passionate. But over time something seems to happen. Things change.

There is a secret to maintaining the passion in emotional, sexual relationships. In moments of attraction and passion, there is an active principle called "sexual polarity." One individual plays the strong masculine pole and one individual plays the strong feminine pole. This creates sexual polarity— an almost irresistible attraction between two people.

The principle of polarity is true in all emotional and sexual relationships, homosexual as well as heterosexual. In fact, we find polarity in all of nature. The masculine and feminine energies are like positive and negative electrical or magnetic qualities. If you have two magnets and put their north and south poles together, they attract each other. Opposite poles attract. But when you flip one magnet around and try to push the two north poles together, they repel. Like poles repel. This same principle of polarity also applies to intimate relationships.

Why Does My Career Turn Him Off?

Few people understand the unique energy of sexual polarity. To maintain sexual polarity, masculine energy must be persistent in its direction, vision, self-discipline and steadiness of love. The feminine energy must be full in its trust, its bodily appreciation of life, its gifts of radiant energy and its willingness to give and receive love. Most importantly, both man and woman must be willing to submit to love and make it their priority.

If you are more directional than your man, it will usually create a problem. If your career is more important to you than his is to him, you will begin to lose your trust in him and he will begin to lose sexual desire for you. This has nothing to do with "should" and "shouldn't": There is nothing wrong with you having a career. It is simply a law of polarity that directionality is a masculine attribute. If yours is stronger than his then the polarity will reverse. You begin to "carry" the masculine energy. This masculine energy in you may begin to repel the masculine energy in your man.

This is a tough concept for people in our culture to handle today, the sacred aspects of our intimate sexual relationships having been lost. Convenience and common financial needs have replaced love-commitment and heart-desire as the motivating forces in many relationships.

It's great to be able to shift between masculine and feminine throughout the day. Both men and women should learn to animate masculine and feminine energy as they need them. But in moments of intimacy, one partner should carry more of the masculine and one partner more of the feminine—if they want ongoing emotional and sexual polarity. Passion neutralizes when partners are not willing to play the masculine and feminine poles in intimate relationship.

Should I Tell Him About My Day?

Does it serve love to talk about your day when both of you come home after work? Or, would it be better to maintain silence, take a bath, and give each other a short massage before saying anything? The art of intimacy involves discovering the specific ways to magnify emotional and sexual polarity and love between you and your partner, not merely as family members or close friends, but as lovers. What would you give to the man to whom you open most deeply, the man who cherishes you not only as a person, but as a woman, as his chosen love?

Why Am I Attracted to Him One Moment and Repulsed the Next?

Imagine that the man is in his masculine energy and the woman is in her feminine. They are attracted to each other. They love each other. All of a sudden, the woman puts out masculine energy. For example, she may say, "Take out the garbage," or, "Let's go out to dinner." These statements are directive or directional. They carry a form of masculine energy and will neutralize the passion between the woman and her man.

In some circumstances, directives are a very effective form of communication. But in a moment of intimacy, when polarity determines attraction, if she tells him what to do it will depolarize their relationship—unless the man wants to carry the feminine energy.

Because he feels her masculine energy, he may begin

treating her like another man. The way a man treats another man is usually not how a woman wants to be treated by her partner. Men challenge each other, compete, analyze and discuss. If you want to be treated as a woman in a moment of intimacy, then be sensitive to whether you are putting out masculine or feminine energy.

The other side is also true. Imagine again that the man is in his masculine energy and the woman is in her feminine. There is a strong attraction between them. They are about to embrace. Suddenly, a huge cockroach jumps out and runs across the floor. The man screams and jumps behind the woman saying, "Oh I *hate* cockroaches, ick! Please kill it, please!" This probably won't cause the woman to be ravenously attracted to him. He has reversed his polarity, dropped his masculine, so to speak. The masculine is more dissociated from life and therefore can kill easier. She'll feel his lack of masculine energy and therefore not be particularly sexually turned on by him.

So it works both ways. In most moments of emotional and sexual intimacy a man wants to receive his woman's feminine energy, and a woman wants to receive her man's masculine loving. If the man decreases his masculine energy, or the woman decreases her feminine energy, then depolarization occurs. Passion diminishes. They may still love each other, but the fullness of their attraction begins to fade.

Depolarization is like flipping one of the magnets around—you become neutralized or even repulsed by one another. During an extreme moment of depolarization you may even begin to feel hate. It's amazing; four seconds ago you were feeling love throughout your body for this person, and now he looks ugly. He turns you off.

When we are polarized with our partner, we can't help but

be attracted. When we are depolarized, we can't help but be bored or even repulsed.

Aren't Some Men Naturally More Feminine?

How much time do you spend with your man each day talking business, going over plans, discussing who is doing what and organizing things? How much time do you spend each day walking barefoot together through the grass smelling the flowers, or making love, leisurely, for hours?

Talking business and organizing plans involves masculine energy. Connecting with the earth and enjoying each other sensually involves feminine energy. In a balanced relationship these two qualities artfully combine throughout the day to magnify love and further personal growth.

The relationship becomes unbalanced, or depolarized, when both partners overemphasize the same side, masculine or feminine. Imagine the man is always saying, "I don't know what to do. Let's just go to the beach." If he says this day after day, year after year, the woman loses trust in him. "Is this it? Going to the beach every day?" The relationship becomes one-sided and she becomes depolarized because he is not incarnating the masculine. The relationship has become lopsided toward the feminine pole.

It can become lopsided toward the masculine too. If the woman is stuck on her masculine energy—constantly talking about business and what has to be done—then the man becomes depolarized and less attracted because he doesn't feel her feminine energy.

If the man prefers to be in his feminine energy, and if the

woman prefers to be in her masculine energy, then the relationship could work in this "reversed" polarity. But this situation is fairly uncommon.

This situation is more common: Many women are naturally more feminine than masculine, but because of stress or professional responsibilities they use predominantly masculine energy throughout the day. Many men are naturally more masculine than feminine, but because of social pressures or childhood experiences they fear their masculine energy. These men use more feminine energy than masculine. In this situation, they are attracted at first, but their sexual polarity decreases as time goes on. Their deep desires are never fulfilled by the compromised energy of a "hardened woman" or a "wimpy man."

He wants to receive her full feminine loving and she wants to receive his full masculine loving. But because of their own tendencies they will not fully incarnate these sexual desires. As sexual characters, they have become compromised by the requirements of their career, the pressures of society, or the history of their childhood.

So they begin to lose trust in one another as intimate partners. They don't receive the kind of love they most need and desire from their partner, masculine or feminine. They lose the passionate attraction to one another that they felt at the beginning. This situation involving a "wimpy man" and a "hardened woman" is much more common in our culture than the naturally feminine man and naturally masculine woman, who are happy living in a "reversed polarity" relationship and turn each other on.

Must I Always Act Feminine If I Want to Be Sexy?

There are times when using your masculine energy is completely healthy, useful and appropriate. Be aware, however, of the consequences. If you have a conversation and both of you are in your masculine energy, don't expect him to treat you like a woman. Don't expect him to be sexually or emotionally attracted to you. Expect him to treat you like a neutral being or like another man.

It is healthy to be as masculine or feminine as you want. This full spectrum is part of any healthy relationship. Both of you might be in your feminine energy, enjoying a luxurious bath together, or in your masculine energy, scheduling the next week. It would be a weird relationship if the woman was never allowed to say anything about plans and the man was never allowed to dance in the garden or cry. This would be another rigid role model for men and women. Just be aware the effect that your masculine or feminine energy is having on the relationship.

People are totally free to move in the full spectrum of sexual energy, masculine and feminine. But if you want passion, then remain conscious of the effect of your energy. It is polarity that creates passion between a man and a woman. You can consciously cultivate and practice sexual polarity in a relationship.

If you have a relationship that has become very business-like, then set aside time to be together as man and woman. Be conscious of how your energy affects your partner moment-to-moment and create the relationship you want. It is only a matter of practice.

Why Do I Enjoy Having Many Men Friends?

The energies of sexuality are such that if you are not receiving masculine energy from your chosen partner you will try to receive it from someone else. Some women aren't with a man, and others don't get enough masculine energy from the man they are with. These women often cultivate male friendships in order to receive masculine energy.

Don't feel guilty for feeling sexually attracted to these men, as well as just wanting to spend time with them. When you are with a man, any man, who is full of masculine energy, you'll feel it. You may be sexually turned on, or maybe just open, happy and receptive. This response is natural.

Men have the same response to women. When men are not receiving enough feminine energy from their partner, or when they are not in an intimate partnership, their sensors automatically open to feminine energy in all its forms. They become healed, turned on and enlivened by women who radiate feminine energy.

The giving and receiving of polarized sexual energy happens naturally. Sexual energy transmits itself naturally, like a flower's perfume carried by the wind. By becoming conscious of the way we give and receive sexual energy even with our friends, we can enjoy each other's gifts of masculine and feminine energy without confusion.

How Does Housework Relate to Passion?

Our intimate relationships have become ambiguous. We expect our partners to be our best friends, able to listen to our

emotional pain. We expect them to be our business col-
leagues, helping us with finances and decisions. We expect
our partners to be housekeepers, childrearers, sex experts and
conversationalists. Our intimacies have become a catch-all
for all of our needs. These unreasonable expectations may
inevitably lead to failure.

If we expect our relationships to work, we must define
what makes our emotional and sexual intimacy unique. I
want my partner to love me, but I also want love from my
close friends, my children and my parents. So what is unique
about the kind of love I want from my intimate partner? How
do I want my intimate partner to touch me, as opposed to the
ways that I want my child or close friends to touch me? We
must define our priorities in intimacy, and stop demanding
that our partner be everything for us.

In general, if you want a good sexual partnership, you cannot expect your partner to be like your same-sex close
friends. As women, you can share your emotions with other
women, truly understand one another, and be healed by such
sharing. But if you try to do the same with your male intimate
partner for too long, you are treating him like a woman
friend, and he may become depolarized. Share your emotions
with your women friends who can more easily resonate with
you, and bring yourself to your intimate partner already
healed by such sharing. Let him heal you and love you in *his*
unique way. Let him heal and love you in the masculine style,
as the most intimate man in your life.

Discover what supports the unique love between you.
When he takes out the garbage and you sweep the floor, can
you embrace each other in love? How about when you take
out the garbage and he sweeps the floor? Find out the details
of a life of love together. As a man, certain activities will

empower him and support his loving and certain activities will weaken him and diffuse his masculine energy. Likewise, as a woman, you may be able to maintain an open heart and body while cooking, but not while arranging payments with the landlord. Who knows? Be sensitive to the effects each activity has on you and your partner. Divide the household activities in a way that supports emotional fullness, sexual polarity and love.

You and your man are much more than housemates. As lovers, the gifts you give to each other are unique.

The way you divide the day-to-day chores between the two of you is one part of the unique way you gift one another, skillfully magnifying your love, sexual polarity and mutual respect.

Isn't It Better to Be Balanced Than All Masculine or All Feminine?

A whole person is able to express both the masculine and feminine, in action and emotion. Such a person can focus and accomplish something without distraction but is also able to relax and engage fully in emotion, feeling and intimacy.

A balanced individual can exercise both masculine and feminine energy. However, for two people to come together as lovers rather than simply business partners or friends, it's good for the man and woman to relax into their masculine and feminine energies, respectively, so that there is a polarity between them.

Culture determines the value placed upon masculine and feminine energy. In our present cultural climate, the masculine is valued more compared to the feminine. Even in our body, in the way we move, we are expected to be more masculine than feminine.

When we are in our feminine there is a kind of relaxed, open, sensual and connected-to-the-elements way of moving. When we are in our masculine there is a kind of angular, on-the-way-to-a-meeting way of moving.

It's much more accepted in our culture to move with purpose and focus. Otherwise it looks as though we're too relaxed, too sensual, too happy. Society determines which style is most accepted, but the style itself is just an expression of the natural masculine or feminine energy. Both styles are necessary for wholeness, but in moments of sexual intimacy, partners need to relax into reciprocal styles if sexual polarity and attraction are to remain alive.

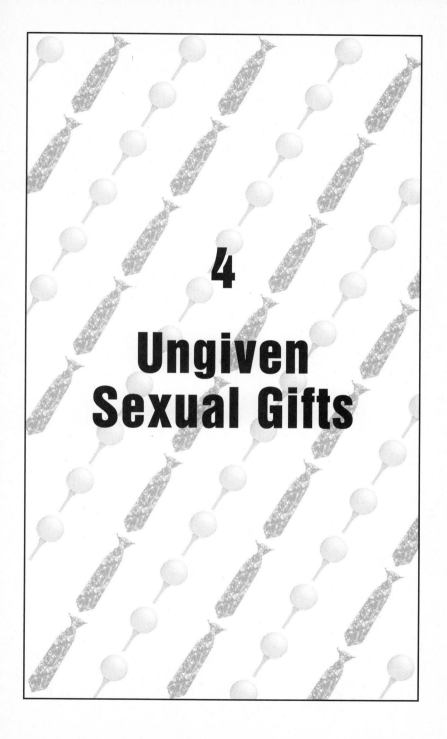

4

Ungiven
Sexual Gifts

Why Are Men Afraid of Women?

The feminine is the ocean, and the masculine is a boat on the ocean. The masculine navigates from one point to another. It takes the ocean currents, the wind and the shifting tides into account in order to reach its destination. The strength of the feminine could crush the masculine at any time. But with skill, the boat can joyfully ride with the ocean's power and achieve a goal. The ocean is all motion, all energy, but doesn't go anywhere specific. The boat can be devoured by the ocean, but it can also move with currents toward a specific place, whereas the ocean flows in many directions at once.

The immensity of feminine energy coupled with the direction of masculine vision result in fullness and balance. Yet the unpredictability and sheer power of feminine energy is daunting to a man who is weak in his vision.

That's why some men say about women, "Can't live with them, can't live without them." To many men, women are the most attractive thing in the world, like a deep blue ocean glistening in the sun. And women are also the most frightening and dangerous, especially when a man feels weak.

The delightfulness of the ocean and its wildness arise from the same vast source of energy. They are both part of the same feminine force. Men are attracted to the spontaneous freshness, the vast, radiant, always changing, unpredictable force of femininity. But they are also repulsed by this force in its wilder form. It requires a strong man, sure of his direction, to embrace a strong woman, full of energy, spontaneity and wildness.

Can a Man Be Strong and Also Feminine?

The whole spectrum of masculine and feminine qualities exists in all of us. On one side of the spectrum is the extreme feminine. It is like walking out in the dew of the garden and dancing in ecstasy, connecting with nature, connecting with life. But it may also be wild and unpredictable.

The extreme masculine, on the other hand, can concentrate on a task to the point of perfection, with no disturbance whatsoever and complete self-discipline. The extreme masculine, in a man or woman, cuts through obstacles and penetrates to the core of the issue, persisting until the final goal is reached.

In between the extreme masculine and extreme feminine is a full spectrum of being. Some of us are comfortable in certain parts of the spectrum but not in others. Very few of us have a free rein throughout the entire spectrum because we may be embarrassed by some aspect of our masculinity or femininity. All of us can learn to be full and whole throughout the spectrum.

For instance, when a man is really enjoying sex, he has a definite directional quality (masculine) as well as a real sensitivity to his partner (feminine). Men who are able to embrace both their feminine and masculine during sex are able to enjoy the sensual as well as the physical experience.

By freeing ourselves to express the entire spectrum, we become more whole as a man or woman. Even so, each of us will find our favorite place in the spectrum. And, each of us will be turned on most by a man or woman who expresses a unique "flavor" of masculine or feminine love.

It's good to be free in our masculine and feminine expression. It's also good to know what we want. Then, we can choose a partner who will not frustrate our desires to imbibe of the more masculine or feminine flavors of loving. We can choose a man or woman who is able to love us in the way that fulfills the yearning in our heart.

Why Don't I Trust My Man When He Just "Hangs Out"?

When the masculine is whole in men or women, they love what they are doing with their lives. They do it with integrity.

When the feminine is whole in men or women, they overflow with love. Their radiance transforms their life and their partner's life. They uninhibitedly give and receive love.

When the masculine is whole, a person becomes a master of conscious doing, a master of vision and direction in life. When the feminine is whole, a person becomes a goddess of love, radiating love into life. Since all of us are both masculine and feminine, we can all become masters of conscious doing and radiant loving.

The feminine part of each of us feels supported when the masculine part of our partner is taking care of life business with clarity and integrity. In the dynamics of a man-woman relationship, if the man hasn't mastered conscious, masculine doing, then the woman has to master it. Because he hasn't cultivated his masculine, his partner may have to overcultivate her own.

When I lived on the Hawaiian island of Kauai, there were quite a few men who were beach bums with very little money. There was a strong tendency for men to be undisciplined in their lives and not master conscious doing because they could just hang out, enjoying the sensuality of Hawaii and remaining in their feminine energy. Therefore, the women on this island became proficient at taking care of themselves quite successfully. Many women on this island had highly developed masculine energy because no man had come into their lives who was trustable.

Naturally, and very healthfully, these women have developed a strong masculine ability to do. This makes it all the harder for them to trust a man because now a man has to come along who is especially good at conscious, masculine doing, since the woman is so especially good herself.

It is difficult for a lost or weakened man to match this kind of woman. For her to truly embrace him as a *man* means that she must feel that his masculine energies are at least as strong as her own. This means she must feel his integrity as a conscious doer: He has a vision of his life. He knows how he is going to accomplish that vision. And, on a daily basis, he is bringing his vision to fruition. This is what the masculine force does in either man or woman.

Is Fairness Always Best?

Certain things that feel like a real gift to you may mean nothing to your man. For instance, most women really love to receive flowers from men. They're seen as a transmission of love. For most men, flowers are nice, but nothing to weep about.

Women and men "speak" a different language of love. After working for years every day with many men and women I noticed that about 80 percent of the women I work with share a language of love and about 80 percent of the men share a language of love. Both languages are distinct and express the specific masculine and feminine feelings about love. But there are always exceptions: Some women may be indifferent to receiving flowers, but not many.

It might be difficult for a man to understand how flowers can make a woman feel so loved, sometimes even to the point of tears. But if a man loves a woman, and he wants his woman to receive his love, he learns to speak love in *her* language. He can learn to give her the gift that most touches her heart.

When we have grown beyond the ideal of constant equality, we can learn how to gift each other in intimacy. When it's no longer an issue who kills the cockroach or who opens the door for whom, we are free to learn each other's language of love. At that point, we can begin to look at who receives the greater gift. If she kills the cockroach, does he feel it as a gift? When he kills the cockroach, does she feel it as a gift? Gifting is rarely perfectly symmetrical. Usually, women and men appreciate giving and receiving different gifts of love.

Over time, we can learn how to express one another's language of love. Then, the relationship fills with life, because we do the specific things that really give each other energy. Either partner could do these things. She is as capable of taking out the garbage as he, but who receives it as a greater gift?

If equality was the main issue, then he would say, "Look, I took out the trash yesterday, so you take it out today." That's fair—but it's not necessarily a gift. So-called fairness is not always the best way to measure a gift.

Once you have achieved fairness in your relationship, once you are no longer clinging to your ideas of roles and "have to's" and "shoulds", then serving one another becomes a matter of gifting, and your gifts to each other are unique.

You might stifle your true motivation to relax a little bit and be honored as a woman because of the notion of fairness or equality, or because you feel you have to do your part and participate in the world, and in your relationship, in a certain way. It's good to honor what you truly desire, deep inside, in the silence of your heart. Then you are able to offer and receive from your partner true gifts, instead of performing according to external roles or because of an internal voice that says you should always be equal in your daily chores. A deep relationship is not a matter of balancing a ledger sheet documenting who did what and when, but a matter of partners first discovering and then giving and receiving their deepest gifts of love.

Who Should Pay for Dinner?

The masculine quality of cherishing and protecting the feminine develops in three stages. In the *first stage* of a relationship, a man wants to cherish and protect his woman. But he also wants to "keep her in her place." She has her role and he has his. "You are a woman, and I want you to act like one. I am a man, and a man acts a certain way." This rigidity is dogma. It becomes something to grow through, something to rise above. This is the first stage.

During the *second stage* of a relationship, equality becomes important. For instance, who pays for the dinner on a date? It used to be that men always bought dinner. Men felt like they "had to." They felt weak if they didn't. It also kept a woman in a certain place and created all sorts of games between the sexes. Our culture soon began to see this as a limitation. It became very positive to break out of these limiting roles, so that men and women on dates both felt free to buy each other dinner—they had equal rights to pay for the date.

It is healthy to grow beyond "shoulds," to grow beyond roles, into this second stage of freedom and equality. You could open the door for your man as well as he could for you. You could pay for his dinner as well as he could pay for yours.

Once equality has been established in a relationship, then we are free to ask, "What is the real gift I can give?" This is the *third stage*, the stage of mutual gifting between men and women, that stage I call "intimate communion." Through which gifts do you best transmit love to each other? Each couple can freely experiment with this.

For instance, most men, when they are acting upon love rather than a "should," feel like they are giving love when they buy their woman dinner or open a door for her. A woman usually receives such a gesture as a gift. It is a way for his masculine "do" mode to express appreciation and honor her feminine radiance.

As long as it doesn't become a role, there are certain things we find that gift each other that are not symmetrical between men and women in every case. For instance, when a woman opens the door for her man, he may appreciate it, but probably doesn't feel anything special. It might as well be a mechanical door.

Ultimately, of course, it doesn't really matter who opens the door or who buys dinner for whom. But it might be worth experimenting to discover who receives it as a real gift of love and who enjoys giving it most.

Are Artists Always Feminine?

Any task done well requires wholeness, a full complement of masculine and feminine energies. Let's look at art as an example. If you are an artist and have too little masculine then you may be very intuitive and very sensitive, but you'll rarely complete a project. If you have too little feminine energy, then you may produce a lot because of your disciplined approach, but you may not be as sensitive to the elements of your medium. A balance of masculine and feminine is required to be creative, sensitive and disciplined as an artist.

Anything done well requires a balance of the masculine and feminine. If you are a high-powered executive, for example, you won't do as well in your job if you don't have a good intuition for people. Being attuned to another's feelings is a feminine quality. Even if you have a very strong organizational ability, you also need sensitivity to people in order to make it as a good executive. The best people in all fields usually have a strong complement of both masculine and feminine energy.

Do I Really Want a Masculine Man?

The religious myths of Hinduism contain a beautiful archetype for the essential masculine and feminine characters. In these myths, God is considered to have a masculine and feminine aspect. The masculine is called Shiva and the feminine is called Shakti.

The masculine is the transcendental aspect. Shiva is totally free yet pervades everything. The feminine aspect, Shakti, is the energy of the universe. Sometimes she is called Parvatti and is considered Shiva's consort. In paintings and sculptures she is shown half-naked with a very curvaceous, feminine body, encircled with jewelry. She wears a gauzy wrap around her waist and legs and is often depicted dancing.

In Hinduism, the play between the masculine and feminine, between Shiva and Shakti, is shown very clearly. The feminine form of God dances and attracts Shiva into life. The masculine form of God pervades through and through everything, including Shakti and her dance. He is attracted into incarnation by Shakti's devotion and radiance.

Just so in everyday life. A Shakti-like woman attracts a man out of his head into his heart. She attracts a man out of his projects and abstract ideals into the reality of life and the relationship of love.

On the other hand, when a woman is lost in her moods, a Shiva-like man's humor and love will lift her out. He will open her out of her moods.

Imagine you are angry. You run into your room and slam the door, telling your man to leave you alone. Your man respects what you say and so he shrugs and walks away. He goes off and finds something to do, or goes out with his friends to let you cool off.

Now imagine, instead, that your man comes into your room and puts his arms around you and looks lovingly into your eyes. You are angry, so you fight against him, push him away, perhaps hit him. But he stays in place with gentle firmness. He quietly tells you with a smile how much he loves you and that he is going to keep holding you, loving you, until he feels you loving him, too.

What kind of man do you want? A man who turns away at

your closed door, or a man who settles for nothing less than love? A fair man, or a Shiva-like man? The choice is up to you.

Why Is It So Difficult for Him to Honor Me As a Woman?

In ancient cultures where women were not obliged to act like men, men and women cherished the feminine. They honored the feminine in a way we don't see today. As women have taken on more masculine characteristics to make it in today's world, both men and women have lost their deep respect for the feminine. They no longer provide the support, integrity and care for a woman that would be natural if both partners trusted and honored the feminine.

In a polarized relationship, a man and woman honor and gift each other. One way that a woman could gift her man is by relieving him of the obligation to be in his feminine too excessively. She gives this gift by relaxing into her feminine energy and doing what she loves to do for him and for herself. Thus, he remains sexually polarized with her, full and strong in his masculine energy. He remains decisive. In order for her to gift him this way, he must relieve her of the obligation to be in her masculine too excessively by providing her with everything she needs to be able to relax into her feminine energy at the appropriate time.

Today, however, the feminine and masculine have been dishonored and degraded. For instance, very few men today are totally connected with a vision that carries them through life with integrity, skill and clarity. They have lost the ability to guide their life from their highest purpose. They have lost touch with their true masculine core, and therefore have trouble honoring you as a woman.

Very few men live a life of conscious completion: "If I were to die today, my life would be complete." As the masculine has degraded, many men have lost their vision. They have lost their ability to say, "This is my highest truth. I want to share it with my woman in love and make it possible in the world."

While many men have lost touch with their masculine sense of direction, many women have lost touch with their bodies. The feminine is very bodily oriented, very sensual and full of life force and pleasure—very alive. Yet the degree to which many women today don't love their own bodies is profound. Your relationship to your body is your relationship to the feminine.

Our culture has allowed a degradation of both the masculine and feminine. It is up to each of us to reclaim the fullness of our sexual character, strengthening our vision and relaxing deeply into our bodies. Then we can honor our partners with our native sexual energies, relieving them of the necessity to be overly masculine or feminine.

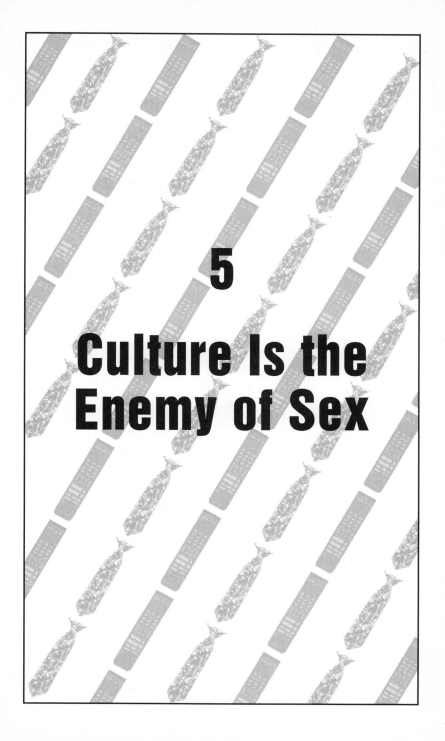

5

Culture Is the Enemy of Sex

Why Does Our Intimacy Seem So Lifeless?

In our culture, there is a very strong bias toward the masculine. Imagine a woman and a man walking down the street, both dressed in suits and carrying briefcases on their way somewhere. This is a common sight in every major city in America. But what if the man and woman were both dancing down the street, singing, touching each other affectionately, sometimes stopping to smell the flowers? This would be a pretty unusual sight.

Even when you go to the beach you don't see everyone in ecstasy, dancing, laughing, rubbing oil on each other's bodies, and celebrating life. But often you do see many people sitting on the beach reading newspapers and books, focused down and using their heads. Our culture is very supportive of the masculine and not very supportive of the feminine, in both men and women.

In our culture you will find many men who are uncomfortable with the feminine aspects of themselves and others. You will also find many women who don't value their own feminine aspects.

Most agriculturally based cultures are sensitive to the flow of the seasons, the elements and nature. In these cultures, men and women both have strong connections to the earth. These cultures are more feminine-oriented. As cultures become more modernized, more daily activity is dissociated from the earth. Work becomes driven by abstract goals and schedules. The culture and its people become more and more masculine-oriented, distancing themselves from the earth and the wisdom of their bodies.

When the individual lives of men and women become

more masculine, so do their intimate relationships. An excessively masculine intimacy seems orderly, dry and lifeless.

When our sexual character becomes distorted by cultural pressures, our intimate relationships suffer. By understanding the masculine and feminine in all of us, we come to understand what makes intimacy work and what makes it fail.

Why Has the Passion Gone Out of Our Relationship?

In traditional cultures, the polarity between men and women was very well understood. It was an artful matter for them to relate to one another without distraction and sexual degradation. Over time, this mutual honoring of sexual differences became dogmatized. It became a rigid and dogmatic approach which kept women and men in their places. It was felt that women should do one thing and men should do another. Rigidly forcing men and women into roles is entirely negative, and the current movement to equalize their access to money, political power and creative expression is very positive.

Yet our culture today has produced quite a few confused and neutralized men and women: passionless men who have difficulty making decisions based on deep vision, and unhappy women who are excessively goal-oriented and more hardened than they would be if they didn't have to live in a masculine-oriented world.

In order to restore passion to our intimate relationships, it is time for men and women to learn how to relax into their full feminine and masculine energy, especially during moments of intimacy. These delicious differences provide emotional and sexual attraction, enchantment, healing and passion between men and women. Without these differences there is no polarity, only two neutralized people wondering where all the passion went.

Can Spending Casual Time with Men Be Harmful to My Sexual Health?

If you spend a lot of time lifting weights, your muscles get bigger. If you spend a lot of time sitting at a desk, your muscles can lose their tone. If you spend a lot of time being with a man, but not *fully* being with a man *in an intimate way*, then your body gets used to that, and it shows. Our bodies and personalities retain our experiences.

For instance, imagine you spend a lot of time working as a waitress in a restaurant where all the men are "hitting on" you, so you put up an energetic sexual defense throughout your workday. This defense remains in your body, emotions, and mind, for several hours after work. In fact, if you put up a defense for too many years, you may develop a chronic disposition of superficial friendliness while cutting off any deeper exchange of sexual energy.

Then you come home to be with your husband. Or perhaps you start a new relationship. And now, even though it is appropriate to be fully sexually polarized with your partner, you have just spent the day, or perhaps many years, being halfway polarized, because it wasn't safe or appropriate to open all the way. It wasn't safe to fully relax and radiate your uninhibited feminine energy. So, now, you bring a halfway feminine energy to your man, and he brings a halfway masculine energy to you. Your sexual characters have become compromised.

When you are attracted to someone, a spiritual energy is released. When you connect with a man, you naturally exchange sexual energies. These energies don't necessarily lead to sexual intercourse, but they are a subtle flow of sexual energy between the two of you.

In our culture, we frequently spend the day intermingling, and maybe even flirting with members of the opposite sex. We express some of our sexual energy, but suppress much of it out of necessity, to guard ourselves and feel more secure.

By suppressing sexual energy and spending a lot of casual time with men, you can inadvertently dampen the passion in your intimate relationship. You bring this habitual closure home to your intimate partner. Doing this day after day can ultimately sabotage your intimate relationship unless you learn how to re-open yourself and relax into your full feminine energy.

How Has Our Culture Changed the Way Men Look at Themselves?

In times of masculine cultural orientation, there is economic and technological growth, political expansion and the destruction of the Earth. In times of feminine cultural orientation, there is a rejuvenation of the Earth and a growth of cooperative politics and historically less technological and economic growth.

Right now we're transitioning from a predominantly masculine-oriented culture to one in which both masculine and feminine are honored. In the process some men have given up their masculine instead of reowning their feminine.

It is almost a *faux pas* for men to be masculine these days. Even the most masculine men belittle themselves in politically correct circles. A little men-bashing and social feminism is considered hip. These days, men are not relaxed in their masculinity. They don't feel as free to do or say what is natural to their core.

Temporarily, a devaluation of the masculine and a revaluation of the feminine may lead to a balance. Hopefully, at some point, we will all be able to be strongly masculine and strongly feminine whenever it is appropriate.

When a culture is one-sided, then androgyny seems like the direction of balance. Androgyny seems superior to a masculine-dominant culture, for instance. What is truly desirable, however, is the full expression of masculine and feminine energies. Why settle for a weak masculine balanced by a weak feminine? Rather, everybody should be free to have highly developed masculine and feminine energies. Then we are free to play in full polarity, enjoying the gifts of strong masculine and strong feminine energies in our intimate relationships.

Is Feminine Energy Less Competent Than Masculine?

The masculine form of competence is the benchmark in our culture. We might presume from this that the feminine is incompetent—but only because it is the masculine form of competence that is given value in our culture.

If our culture was more feminine-oriented, we would value loving relationships, creating and sustaining life, healing each other and the Earth, and freeing the emotions. Based on this feminine benchmark, masculine energy is quite incompetent. Whatever we value most will color our sense of what is competent and vice versa.

It is impossible for you to value the feminine as long as you assume it is incompetent. And it is also impossible for your man to be fully attracted to you as a woman. Your man will not be able to relax in his support of you as long you feel that what you have to offer is not worthwhile.

Men and women in our culture are raised with this false judgment of feminine energy. Analytical ability, financial "swordsmanship" and entrepreneurship; these are considered forms of competency. This domain of competition and mentality is not the natural domain of the feminine. It is the natural domain of the masculine, and we are in a masculine-oriented culture.

As you begin to relax into your feminine energy, you may hear an inner voice: "Don't relax too much. You will become incompetent." This voice is society's voice ingrained into you as an individual. All the work we are doing to re-incorporate the feminine balance in our society at the political, economic and cultural level is good, but it won't change much unless we also change at the individual level and revalue our feminine power of life and love.

Why Do I Feel Silly Around My Lover?

When a woman is in a polarized relationship with a man, his masculine energy may polarize her more fully into her extreme feminine. One of the qualities of the extreme feminine is mindlessness, in a positive sense. Whenever you are totally involved in your body, in love, in your senses, or in another person's energy, you are mindless. For instance, if you are giving or receiving a great massage, or making love passionately, you are totally connected with someone, and you are basically mindless; you are connected through means other than the mind. If you are not used to this state of open flow and feeling you may feel "silly."

The feminine in each of us is, in essence, mindless, though not stupid or silly at all. It is supremely intelligent with the wisdom of the body, a subtle connection with the flow of energy and deep intuition. The more men and women allow themselves to be in their feminine, the more they experience intuitive empathy rather than analytic mind chatter.

Of course, people have resistance to this. Our culture is so masculine-oriented that we think we are stupid or silly if we don't have thoughts, opinions and ideas running through our mind. Whereas, in fact, a quiet mind is rather free and able to be alert and present.

In our feminine energy, we resonate fully with others. And this is very valuable. Some people struggle all their lives just to free themselves of enough personal subjectivity so they can be fully present with their partner instead of stuck in their heads.

There is a time to be thinking and a time to be feeling. Before we can fully trust our own feminine energy, we must understand that thoughtless feeling is not inferior to analytical thinking. The feminine is not "silly," though it may be mindlessly ecstatic or intuitively connected, without a single thought to interfere.

How Can Men Strengthen Their Masculine and Women Strengthen Their Feminine?

In our modern society, we lack a coherent masculine culture wherein men get together with other men and keep each other aligned to truth: "Hey friend, wake up." Men need this, otherwise they become weak and ambiguous: "I don't know what I'm going to do. Maybe I'll have a beer." Without a strong men's culture, men become unclear, indecisive and ambiguous about the direction of their lives.

Shared masculine energy offers men challenge, an edge of responsibility and discipline. Without this energy they tend to flounder and lose their sense of inner truth. As a woman, you cannot take the responsibility to rebuild and refocus your man's masculine energy. He does that on his own and with other men.

Likewise, our society lacks a strong women's culture. One of the best ways for a woman to nurture and strengthen herself is in the company of other women. A group of women shares something that just doesn't happen when a man is present. Women can relax together, let their hair down, nurture one another, dance together, soften their masculine edge and breathe freely. The feminine is nourished in the company of other women.

For a sexually polarized relationship to remain fresh and alive, it is necessary for the man to spend substantial time with other men, and for the woman to spend substantial time with other women. This way, their masculine and feminine essences remain strong, clear and full, able to polarize one another in the play of sexual and emotional intimacy.

6

Understanding the Drama of Woman and Man

Will We Ever Stop Hurting Each Other?

The ongoing play between man and woman looks like this: At times, the man leaves, and the woman's love and radiance attracts him back into the relationship. At other times, the woman gets lost in moods of longing and emotions, of hurt and rejection, and the man draws her out into the relationship with humor, perspective and happiness. These are only two aspects of the essential emotional drama between men and women.

You may sometimes get lost in moods of hurt, longing and doubt. If he is a good man, your partner will gift you with loving humor and perspective. He will communicate, "I love you," opening you into heartful connection and relaxed, intimate communion. That's one of his masculine gifts to you.

At other times, he will get distracted, pulling out of life and the relationship. If you are a good woman, you will invite him back with your love and radiance, attracting him into the relationship, giving him life and energy. That's one of your feminine gifts to him.

In archetypal gifting, the feminine invites the masculine into love, dances in love for him, feeds him with love and gifts him with her personal energy. The masculine gifts the feminine with strong and gentle loving that goes right through you, penetrating deep into your heart, opening you into happiness, humor and love.

This mutual gifting is a central feature of a mature intimacy. Rather than turning away, man and woman learn to give love, even when they feel hurt by each other's actions.

What Happened to the Juice?

One reason intimate relationships become less passionate over time is that they become more and more practical and business- or family-oriented. The man and woman become less and less relaxed in their masculine and feminine poles. Therefore, sexual polarity decreases. But it doesn't have to be that way.

Men cannot resist true feminine radiance. Most women know that if they really shine their feminine energy, they could have men wrapped around their little fingers. By being very feminine, virtually every man who comes into their personal sphere will be attracted to them.

The opposite is also true. If a man is really present, really charismatic in a positive sense, full of masculine force and confident passion, he is very attractive to most women. If the other men in the room are kind of wishy-washy and wimpy, then a man who is full of masculine charisma is going to stand out.

In social situations, men and women need to be responsible for their masculine and feminine energy. That is, in certain social situations you may not want to animate energies that will polarize and tease all the men (or women) in the room.

But intimate relationships are different. To achieve deep emotional and sexual intimacy, women and men must incarnate deep feminine and deep masculine energy in the play of their relationship together. If you are not doing this, your relationship may become more businesslike and practical. In other words—depolarized. It loses the passionate dynamic. The "juice" dries up.

To repolarize, try this: Be the goddess your man would love to spend his evening with. Realize that, as a man, he tends to move out of relationship. He's always moving toward the realm of abstraction, of newspapers, TV and his own mind. It's your gift to be the goddess, to be the feminine dancer of love that awakens his heart and draws him into the dance of life with you.

You may have to move through personal resistance to love so fully. He may need to move through his own resistance to incarnate and commit to the masculine form of love. Such depth of love is not accomplished once and for all in an instant. But each of you can consciously practice in that direction, supporting each other as you grow in your ability to give love. Over time, you grow to fully embody the gifts of masculine and feminine loving.

You frequently discover that, in fact, you actually want to be the person your partner wants you to be. Not for him, but for yourself. The person he wants you to be is often the person that *you* want you to be. By learning to gift your partner with love, you are actually learning to give your highest gift to yourself as well. We are born here to learn to love—not for our partner's sake, but for the sake of love itself. Loving is its own reward.

What Does He Really Want from Me?

The reason a man chooses to be with a *woman* as an intimate partner—rather than with another man, a cat, or nobody— is because he wants to be intimate with the feminine force of the universe. He's choosing to open himself in intimacy with someone who can give him *feminine* love and energy; that's why he's chosen a *woman* for an intimate partner.

If you remember that your man has chosen you as a *woman* because he wants feminine energy, then you will always know the key to waking him up and attracting him into relationship.

If he's reading the newspaper it's probably because the newspaper is the most attractive thing for him in that moment. Since men are modal, they can shift themselves into the realm of news rather quickly. It's euphoric in a sense, because everything else disappears. His burdens are temporarily relieved.

The special energy you can uniquely offer him in that moment is feminine love. However, if you are angry or hurt, you may want to rip up the newspaper and say "Goddamnit, you're always reading the stupid newspaper!" Rather than that, you could try leaning over and kissing him. Maybe stand behind him and massage his shoulders a little bit. It's going to take a really rigid man to sit there looking at the newspaper and not put it down while you are massaging his shoulders— and some men are that rigid.

A key for the woman's side of the relationship is acknowledging her power of feminine attraction. Because many men tend to be so rigid and stuck in their self-centered world, they need to be attracted by the feminine force. Their rigidity is healed by that force. And then they open in love. When you are in touch with your love, in touch with your heart, and when you offer him your love as a woman, he will be attracted beyond his momentary form of self-involvement or distraction.

The feminine force is a gift that gives energy and life—for instance, putting on really nice music and dancing, giving a simple massage or bringing him a glass of juice in the morning. Your feminine energy makes him feel, "Ahhh. It's great to be alive and with you." The feminine form of love is a gift that enlivens him.

It could be your smile. It could be the beautiful clothes you wear—or don't wear. It could be the way you put flowers next to the bed. It could be the way you whisper your love to him. It could be anything that has the effect of relieving his sense of burden and bringing him life energy.

Whereas the feminine feels blessed by life and relationships, most men feel burdened. Women feel equally burdened by life and relationships if they are in their masculine mode. The sense of being unburdened, of delight, of energy, of radiance, of enlivenment, of the flow of life itself, is feminine energy. And it comes from your heart of love. When you gift a man with this energy of love he feels you as his cherished woman, rather than a housemaid, a business partner, or a mother. He feels you as a goddess.

For a satisfying intimacy, of course, men must also know how to give feminine energy and women must know how to give masculine energy. But most men are looking for the feminine form of love in intimate relationship, most of the time. Otherwise they might have chosen a gay relationship or a relationship with a very masculine woman. Or perhaps they would have chosen no intimate relationship at all.

Should a Man Obey His Woman?

If a man meekly obeyed his woman, if he just said, "Oh, anything you say, dear," then he would not be incarnating the masculine force in relationship. Most women aren't turned on by a man who always does anything she says. Women innately know that only a man with his own true vision is strong enough to love her the way she really wants to be loved.

On the other hand, in a relationship, a man learns to submit himself to heart-responsibility, to commitment in love, and yields his self-centeredness in his practice of intimacy.

In love, you don't give yourself up as if you were weak, rather, you allow yourself to be submitted wholeheartedly to the process of love.

How Do I Attract a Strong Man?

Men tend to be weak in their emotional life. Your man may be stuck in his head, stuck in his projects, stuck in his purpose. His emotional life may be dry and empty. You are his source of radiance and delight. You are his source of wild energy. As his chosen woman, you are his most intimate source of the feminine force of the universe. This is your unique gift to him, if you choose to gift him with your feminine love.

On the other hand, women tend to be weaker in aligning their actions with their highest vision. They may allow their emotional state to over-influence the clarity and direction of their actions. If you feel closed, for instance, it's often hard to open even though you know in your heart that love is better than withdrawal. Or, you may know in your heart that it's time to change jobs, but still find it difficult to take the next step. The masculine is good at helping the feminine live its highest purpose. The source of this masculine energy of organization and direction may be your man or your own masculine energy.

If you are weak in your self-discipline, if you have difficulty deciding on and achieving your goals, then you need
more masculine energy in your life. You can develop your
own masculine energy by learning to set goals, following
schedules, meeting deadlines and disciplining your daily
activities.

You don't have to balance yourself first. You can gift each
other in a relationship, and by doing that, you achieve balance.
You are balanced by him and he is balanced by you. For
instance, his mental goal-orientation can be balanced by your
intuitive sensitivity. Your wild energy and emotional flow can
be balanced by his stability, discrimination and humor.

How do you attract an intelligent, strong, playful man? To
attract full masculine energy you must be relaxed in your
body as a woman, as the full feminine incarnation of the universe. You must trust that the feminine side of yourself is not
stupid, inadequate or weak. When you fully honor your feminine, then you will attract a man who honors your feminine
as you do. You will be able to come together and serve one
another.

Of course, if you are naturally strong in your masculine
energy, you may not want a man with a strong masculine
force and a desire to cherish and care for you as his feminine
source of love. Your self-discipline and organizational abilities may be fully developed already, and you may not want a
man who enters your life with his masculine energy. It is up
to you. You may prefer a man who gives you more feminine,
nurturing, supportive love.

If you want a man who will gift you with strong masculine
integrity, passion and humor, then relax in your feminine
energy and you will attract him. If you want a man who will
not interfere with your life as it is, who will not make loving

demands of you so much as offer emotional support and acceptance, then animate your more controlling, directive, masculine energy. The man you attract will appreciate receiving your guidance and direction. Rather than penetrating your life with masculine love he is more likely to give you feminine, nurturing love with very little direction of his own.

The choice is up to you. Just remember that you always will attract a man who puts out energy reciprocal to that which you are putting out, masculine or feminine.

Who Gets to Make the Decisions, Him or Me?

Decisions about what to do are an "even deal" between people. But they are not an even deal between masculine energy and feminine energy. The feminine energy gets what it wants in love. The masculine energy gets what it wants in freedom. Your partner cannot be full in his masculine energy and also give up freedom for your preferences. You cannot be full in your feminine energy and also give up love for his preferences.

For instance, imagine you want to move to one city and he wants to move to another. Because love is the priority for the feminine, you have the potential to stay in your feminine energy, giving and receiving love with him, and yet not live in the place you would choose, because that's secondary to the feminine. Where you live is less important than if you share deep love, if you are in your feminine energy.

But for the masculine, if forced to choose, freedom is more important than love. So if your man feels an ultimatum from you—he has to live where you prefer or else he loses you—

then he is going to feel your masculine choice. Your priority is your career, your freedom or whatever it is that makes you want to live in a particular place.

This is fine, but realize that you are prioritizing freedom above love. You are choosing your masculine priority over your feminine priority. This choice will inevitably depolarize the relationship, unless you are with a man who prefers to gift you with feminine, rather than masculine, energy.

What Can Men and Women Learn from Each Other?

Women often have to teach men how to incarnate love in a relationship. On the other hand, men often teach women how to be free.

You would be doomed if you were only happy in a relationship because all relationships end. You would also be doomed if you could not love in relationship, since life consists of relationship. Therefore, each of us needs to learn the masculine lesson of freedom prior to relationship and the feminine lesson of love in relationship.

Women teach men life and men teach women death. They are both necessary lessons. A good man teaches how to let go of emotionally binding attachments. A good woman teaches how to love within a relationship, within a commitment. His freedom can teach her not to cling. Her love can teach him to surrender his self-centered distraction.

Why Do Men Balk at Commitment?

Men tend to argue for the possibility of love without real commitment. In response to men's ideas about possible relationships, women often feel, *I'm real. Don't give me your theoretical bullshit. You're either loving me right now or you're not.* She wants concrete love. *Don't give me any of your heady philosophy. I'm not feeling your love right now. You're not incarnating love right now.* She tests whether her man is really loving, or just thinking of love. *I am here. I am real. Love me.* She is here to love.

The man says, "I know you really want my attention, but can you feel love whether I am here or not? Can you be free and happy whether anything is here or not?" This is the masculine teaching of love.

The more full the masculine and feminine teachings of love are, the more close they come to being the same. At the meeting point, there is no difference between the masculine and the feminine. There is no difference between freedom and love. Since true love is all-encompassing, resisting nothing, it is totally free. And, since real freedom is fearless, with no sense of threatened self, it is completely loving. Freedom and love, masculine and feminine, are not different in their full fruition.

Yet there tends to be a concrete difference at the human level. The masculine is more able to stand outside of things and point out, "You are in a mood right now. This is just a mood. Remember love. In this moment, there is nothing preventing you. You don't need this and that. You don't need anything. Just remember love right now." This is the masculine gift.

The feminine gift is like the sound of a ringing bell, a reminder of love in life. "Hey, you! You are distracted in your theories and projects and TV. This is where love is expressed, with me. Right here. I'm here to be loved. I'm here loving you." The feminine calls the masculine into the beauty of life and the embrace of love.

We need both these gifts. Without the full masculine and feminine, we become weakened. One feminine weakness is to feel, *Unless I'm married, unless I'm in a long-term intimate relationship, I can't really experience love.* One masculine weakness is to think, *Well, if we get married I can't be free. I don't want to limit my life. I don't want to be trapped.*

When we are balanced with ourselves and in our relationships, we are free to give our love without fearing dependency, loss of self or confinement. We are free *and* we are loving. If our relationship ends tomorrow, fine—today we give each other love. If our relationship lasts a lifetime, fine—today we give each other love.

Why Is So Much Emphasis Placed on a Woman's Attractiveness?

The masculine and feminine forces of the universe are evident in religious and spiritual archetypes the world over. In Hinduism, as mentioned earlier, the one Divine Being is conceived to have two aspects: Shiva and Shakti, man and woman or masculine and feminine energies. Shakti is the feminine energy.

Shakti attracts Shiva, the masculine form of the Divine, into incarnation. The divine play in Hinduism is the incarnation of the transcendental aspect of the Divine, or the masculine aspect, into life, attracted by the feminine aspect of the Divine.

The story of Jesus is another example of this divine process. Jesus's play with women, with Mary, was about incarnating as a human. In the book and movie, *The Last Temptation of Christ*, this is portrayed vividly. Since it is told from a patriarchally biased perspective, however, Jesus's attraction to women is seen as evil. In the Adam and Eve myth also, it is the woman who invites the man with the apple, the fruit, the life.

The feminine attracts the masculine into life and love. That's the spiritual function, so to speak, of the feminine aspect of the Divine with respect to the masculine: to attract the masculine into life, into love.

You could be whole as a *person* without doing this, but to be whole as a *woman* in emotional and sexual intimacy with a man, you have to be comfortable in the role of attracting the masculine into life and love. Embodying the feminine pole of relationship means to be connected to your heart, breathing love in and out of your whole body, giving and receiving love with your man, and creatively using your energy in a way which attracts the masculine into life, love and relational enjoyment.

The masculine is the opposite, or really the complement, of the feminine. It's the transcendental aspect of the Divine that is free of the motion of life. The masculine brings insight, perspective and humor when the feminine is lost. When life seems confusing, when you are lost in a mood, it's the masculine that stands free of confusion, embraces you unconditionally, and says, "I love you." The masculine penetrates through your shell of emotional closure and opens your heart with passion, playfulness and integrity. The masculine brings you out of the complexity of emotions into the simplicity of love. It is a transcendental awakening into freedom.

The masculine gives the gift of transcendental awakening. The feminine gives the gifts of life energy and love. Together, the two are consummated in transcendental love. In the drama of intimacy, the play of the feminine with respect to the masculine is the attraction of the masculine into life through love. That's the greatest gift you could give your man.

You might choose not to do that, and that's fine. You may prefer to give your love in a more neutral, or even masculine, way. However, there is a difference between free choice and suppression. Especially in today's culture, the whole feminine way of being is suppressed and criticized. It's very difficult for men and women in our culture to allow themselves to relax in their feminine energy.

In our culture today, feminine attractiveness is sometimes considered suspect. But attraction is a key element of the feminine force. It's not merely physical attraction, although that's a part of it. The attractive elements of the feminine force include radiance, sensuality, love, healing, spontaneous delight and creative energy. We all must learn to honor this part of ourselves.

As a woman, the more you are able to allow yourself to relax into your feminine dimension, the more you will attract a man who will reciprocate with his masculine strength. He will be full in his masculine integrity, direction, humor, passion and persistence in love. And he will honor you as an embodiment of the feminine force of the Divine.

7

Dealing with a
Difficult Man

Why Do Men Always Blame Women?

To many men, the feminine is a force of distraction and any time a man is not fully living his vision he will blame it on his woman. Men have blamed women for virtually every negative circumstance on Earth, including lack of spiritual growth. In Hindu mythology, for instance, the force of distraction and illusion, Maya, is depicted as a woman.

For many men, women are either glorious goddesses or evil sirens. Women are either the gift of radiance or a distraction. Men can switch from one of these perspectives to the other very quickly. When your man switches from seeing you as a goddess to seeing you as a distraction, it doesn't feel good.

You will notice that your man typically treats you as one or the other. He will say, "I love you. You are everything." Or, he will be resentful, "You are distracting me from this. I give my attention to you instead of my work. Leave me alone. You are a burden to me."

This attitude is not unique to your relationship. Men resent women as distractions universally. Men cannot help, for instance, but be distracted by a radiant woman when she walks into the room. If a group of men are sitting around talking and a radiant woman walks in, things shift—their attention goes to the woman. It's automatic. They are sexually polarized to her. Even when they are not going to act it out, an energetic sexual attraction and arousal occurs in most men many times a day. So men have an inherent distrust of the feminine—when there is a woman around, they are not going to be able to focus on their job. Their mind will not be clear.

Time and time again, your man will blame you for any lack of clarity he feels. Even if you are totally supportive but he is not strong enough to live his vision, he will still blame you. He will look at you and imagine he is constrained or compromised by your relationship together. He will resent you. It's amazing how often this happens.

It's up to your man to cultivate his masculine energy, becoming strong in his clarity and vision. You can't help him directly with this process. But you can continue loving and growing. You want to live your life in love, whether you stay with this partner or find a new one. When a man and woman are really committed to the practice of love in intimacy, they can suffer each other's insults and continue growing.

Why Isn't My Man More Self-Directed?

Some men have been told all their lives not to tell others what to do. Perhaps their parents inhibited their behavior. Perhaps they observed how family members were hurt by their father's directiveness. Men like this have a tough time knowing their direction. As soon as they are ready to move they wonder, "Is it safe? Will I still be loved? Am I going to hurt someone?" They live their lives meekly because they don't allow themselves to incarnate their full masculinity. And that includes a confident sense of direction.

Sometimes a woman inadvertently weakens her man's masculine energy. For instance, suppose your man is out in the world with his "sword." He may be trying to make money. He may be absorbed in a creative project. He may be intensely practicing his spiritual exercises. Or he may be lifting weights. Regardless of what he is doing, he is very directed and very purposed.

You feel his attention absorbed in something other than you. You may say, "You are always working. You are always doing this, always doing that." What he feels is, *She doesn't like me the way I am, as a man.* He feels as if you are criticizing his masculine energy.

If he feels that you are hurt by his masculine focus, he may suppress his masculine energy to try and give you the attention he thinks you want. But this never works; when he diminishes his masculine energy he also depolarizes the relationship.

When you feel him absorbed in a project, try to gift him with your sensitivity by allowing yourself to feel into his life. Is your man following his heart's desire? Is he not paying attention to you because he is focused on living his truth, or is he just being selfish? Allow him to follow his truth, but let him know when his selfishness hurts you. Temper his sword with your heart, but do not inadvertently condemn his masculine energy. If he tries to curb his need to follow his vision because he is afraid of your response, he will only weaken his sexual essence.

If your man lacks self-direction, his masculine energy has probably become weakened or suppressed. This suppression may have happened during his childhood, or it may be occurring right now in your relationship. He must find, and align himself with, his own sense of direction. All you can really do for him is be aware of how your communications affect him. Are you empowering his masculine, or do your communications inadvertently cause him to weaken his sense of direction?

Why Do I Attract Lazy Men?

Sometimes your man's masculine way of focusing on his projects and work hurts you. But at other times you are hurt by his lack of masculine energy. Let's assume your man lazily watches TV all the time and has no real direction in his life. How did you end up with a man who has so little directional masculine energy?

In most cases, a woman who has strong masculine energy would attract, and be attracted to, a man who has weakened masculine energy. If a more feminine woman got close to him, she wouldn't feel much masculine strength and probably wouldn't be attracted to him. However, a woman who possesses strong masculine energy would be attracted to a man with a weak masculine because his masculine energy would not overpower (or interfere, or detract) from her masculine energy.

If you have chosen a man who does not have strong direction, try to examine your unconscious reasons for choosing such a man. Do you want to have your own way? Do you also want to be ravished by a man who loves you? You invite strong masculine love by relaxing in your strong feminine love, trusting your man's directionality and inviting him into the realm of feeling with an open heart—without giving up your own true direction.

What Can I Do When His Sex Drive Suddenly Disappears?

If anything interrupts your man's directionality, he will feel emasculated. His feeling of weakness will then affect his sexual drive and his passion toward you as a woman, because he has become depolarized as a man.

A man's sense of self-worth is deeply connected to his ability to persist or carry through with a goal. For instance, he is trying to write a novel and he can't do it. He is trying to make money and something falls through. These kinds of things are more important for most men than their intimate relationships.

For most women, the success of their intimate relationship is at the core of their life in one form or another. They also have many other aspects to their lives, but love or the lack of love is the main concern at the feminine core.

For most men, however, their quest, purpose or mission is at their core. An intimate relationship may be an extremely important part of a man's life, but at the core of his life is his quest—his quest for money, creativity, God or whatever. This quest takes precedence over everything else for the masculine.

It is very natural for you to feel hurt, rejected, abandoned or unloved when he is not paying attention or giving you the energy that you want. Remember, though, that if he is not there for you it may be because his life quest is failing. Remember also that unless a man is succeeding in his purpose, he is not capable of being in a full relationship with you, and he cannot offer you his love fully. Instead, the energy he would otherwise give to you is sucked into his hollow core.

You will feel this as a collapse, a collapse away from you.

But if you could feel it from his point of view you would feel it as a collapse into the hollow core of his failing life.

Once you understand what your man is feeling, you will begin to accept your man's withdrawal. Realize that it's not your fault. Realize that even if you were the perfect woman, even if you were doing everything "right," whatever that means, he still could not be there for you if his personal quest was failing.

If he feels like he is supposed to have energy for you even though his core is failing, he will begin to feel guilty. He will feel bad because he is not doing what he should do in the relationship with you. This added demand will begin to wear on him. Finally, he may come to the point of wanting to reject everything.

He may finally break down and say, "I can't take your demands anymore." You may feel, *I'm not demanding anything! I'm only supporting you.* But he feels you as a demand. He is, in fact, inventing the demand. He feels, *The core of my life is collapsing and I'm supposed to be here for you. You are placing this demand on me.* It feels like a demand to him even though you don't demand it. He feels, *I have to be there for my wife. I have to be there for my children. I have to mow the lawn. And here at the core of my life I'm feeling totally devastated.*

Traditionally, in cultures that had more wisdom than our present culture, a man in this state would go on a vision quest. He would seek a vision that would guide his life, then he would align his life with this vision. How did a man engage in such a quest traditionally? He would do it alone or in the company of other men. Such a quest does not traditionally involve women.

During difficult times, you will find that your man has a

desire to spend time alone or with his men friends rather than with you. At this point in his life, more important than anything else, he must try to get his life together by finding his vision and aligning his life with it.

First, he needs to decide what his vision is. Then he must set up his life so that for a period of time he does nothing else except align his life with his vision. In this culture, finding his vision may not be possible because he is expected to do things like go to work and take care of household projects. In other cultures, the vision quest takes priority: Your man would be expected to forgo his responsibilities to complete his quest. As in other cultures, your man needs to dedicate as much life-energy as possible to discovering and aligning his life with his vision.

Part of this will probably involve a temporary retreat from your relationship in some form. Perhaps your man could move into a separate room, with the understanding that for the next day, or next week, he is not going to be responsible for the children or the household duties. Perhaps you could hire someone to help. There are ways to work around it.

It might take a day, it might take a week, but eventually he will begin to realign his life. And when he does he will feel his natural and true masculinity. A man only feels masculine when he is aligned with his direction. When he loses his vision, or when he loses his ability to live his vision, it is as if he becomes impotent, physically as well as emotionally.

You can help your man align himself with his vision by eliminating distractions from his life and helping him live his freedom, his creativity, his quest.

Why Can't He Express His Appreciation for Me?

Anything you do that serves your man's quest feels like a gift to him. Anything you do that obstructs his quest feels like a slap in the face.

Most important to the feminine is love, but most important to the masculine is freedom. As a woman, you may assume that when you gift your man with a glass of water, what he feels is love. But that's not the entire gift he receives. He does feel your love. However, the gift that you bring to a man— what feels most like your special gift of feminine energy to him—is not the emotion of love *per se*, but the freedom and the energy it gives him. When you bring him a glass of water, your energy frees him to continue his quest.

One reason your man might not express his appreciation when you do something for him is that if he has to break away from what he is doing to express his appreciation, then it is no longer such a gift. If he has to stop what he's doing, if he has to leave his train of action and thought and turn to you and exchange acknowledgment, this can often pull him off the track of his quest.

If expressing his appreciation for your action takes him away from his quest, then your gesture is no longer such a gift in his experience. Of course, once his quest has been set aside, he's a fool if he doesn't completely express his appreciation to you in some way. However, if you expect your man to express his appreciation during his focus, you are setting yourself up for disappointment.

If he is obliged to break his quest to express appreciation to you, he may resent you. In some insidious fashion, he will express his resentment towards you even while he expresses appreciation.

Don't expect your man to always stop what he is doing to express his appreciation. In the long run, however, you will know his appreciation. You have gifted him in a way that nobody else can. He feels your unique gifts of love. Through your gifts, you give him freedom. Through his gifts, he will give you love. If he doesn't, you are with the wrong man.

How Can I Reach Him Without Making Him Angry?

The male and female relationship is good for balancing the extremes of the masculine and feminine. Nothing balances a man's dry rigidness more than the love of a woman. And nothing balances a woman's sensitive emotions more than a man's love. Men and women can balance and serve one another this way.

Just because the masculine character is modal, or one-pointed, doesn't mean that you should tolerate him when he is just acting like a stubborn child or avoiding something.

Know that most men are modal. It's a masculine quality that should be honored. But you should also question whether his life is being served by his modality in this moment, or is he lost in his own narrow mind.

If you honestly feel he's not being served, that he's just rigidly stuck in a selfish mode, then you could serve him with your feminine energy. This doesn't mean arguing with him or analyzing him. Instead, you might want to put your hand on his shoulder and say, "Hi." Or, "It's a beautiful day." Bring him into his body with your touch. Soften his edges with the loving tone of your voice. Enliven his dry heart with the sweet force of your feminine energy. Find out what works.

It's really an art to heal each other in intimacy.

You will know what to do from your heart when you no longer fall into the trap of being hurt by him or pushing him away. If he is self-absorbed, you might feel hurt, abandoned, or rejected. You might also react by punishing him in kind: "If he doesn't want to pay attention to me, I'm not going to pay attention to him." When you go beyond a reactive response, you will be able to feel what he needs and help him snap out of his little world to rejoin you in intimate connection.

He is already in his modal, masculine energy. The secret is to connect to him through the polarity of your feminine energy. If you put out masculine energy, instead—discussing his "problem" with him, or analyzing him—then he will only be depolarized further away from intimacy. However, the polarity of your feminine energy will attract him into your healing, if he is able to receive you. All you can do is offer your gift. Whether he receives it or not is up to him.

Why Is He So Afraid of Getting Close?

Men fear constraint. Remember that! The closer they get to being completely attracted by you, the more they feel, "Whoah! I'm going to lose my freedom." The more their attraction to a committed relationship grows, the more they will talk about wanting their freedom.

Especially at the beginning of a relationship, men feel themselves slipping from the freedom of bachelorhood into the constraint of relationship. They say things like, "My business is important to me and I need to spend a lot of time with it." Or, "We might be getting close, but don't get the idea that we are going to see each other every day. I need a lot of time by myself."

He is trying to convince himself: "No, I'm not going to lose my own life. No, I'm not going to lose my freedom." The more he feels love drawing you together, the more reasons he will give as to why he needs his freedom and the ways he will keep his freedom. He will talk about his freedom because he's feeling attracted to you—he is precisely *not* rejecting you, although that may be what it feels like to you.

The times he is most afraid of commitment usually come after periods of incredible intimacy. You will have a really intimate time together, and the next morning he says, "I think we should spend some time apart."

You feel, "We just had this incredibly intimate time together. What's wrong? Did I do something wrong? Is it over? What's happening?"

Perhaps what he is really trying to say is, "Intimacy scares me because I'm afraid of losing my freedom." It's an acknowledgment of intimacy. It's an acknowledgment of love, expressed as, "Wait a minute. Let's take a break."

The fullest possible response on your part is to feel whether the space or freedom he asks for serves him or not. If it serves him, then transcend your own sense of hurt and rejection, and allow your heart to remain open to love.

If he chooses his freedom over committing to you, that's his choice. You can only provide him with an invitation into love. Then you will find his natural rhythm of needing time apart and wanting to be with you, as well as your own rhythm. This practice of continuing to be present in love when you feel rejected, rather than pulling away and feeling insulted, moves you out of the cycle of emotional reactivity. This cycle goes nowhere: He expresses his need to be apart, you feel hurt, withdraw, and then he feels hurt, unattracted, and likewise withdraws further. This cycle is endless, unless one of you is willing to give love even while you feel hurt.

So, discriminate why he is pulling away. Perhaps he is being a jerk, but maybe his fears are genuine and he needs time to open up to love you. Before you automatically shut down, decide if his needs are real.

Why Does Intimacy Seem Less Important to Him Than to Me?

If a man doesn't feel he is living his vision completely, he cannot give his full love. A woman usually has the ability to love in intimacy, and also master her "doing," at the same time. Men, however, often must master doing *first* in order to have the free energy and attention to love. Otherwise, he is full of self-doubt and feels his woman is a constraint and a demand. His woman's mere presence demands his attention, and he will resent her for drawing him away from his quest, his search, his vision.

When the masculine principle is whole in your man, he loves what he is doing. He does it with integrity. And when he is with you, this sense of wholeness allows him to be fully with you. His attention isn't compromised by a nagging sense of having unfinished business in other areas of his life.

It is the ultimate castration for a man not to be able to follow his vision because of his woman. Even if he has willingly made this choice, it feels like emasculation to him. It is impossible for a man to be sexually polarized with the woman for whom he has given up his vision. This choice is the exact opposite of what the masculine energy is all about.

It is impossible for a man to feel whole and give you passionate love if he gives up his vision in order to be with you. He might, however, have to sacrifice personal preferences and little things he wants in order to make the relationship work. That's not the same as sacrificing his vision of what his life is about.

Freedom to a man is what love is to a woman. For him to sacrifice his freedom, his vision of life, in order to be with you, means giving up his most essential desire. The equivalent for you as a woman would be to give up your desire to experience love. Would you be willing to give up experiencing love in order to be in relationship with your man? That would be ridiculous. You are with him in order to experience love. And he is with you to experience love, which he can only do fully when he is free to pursue his true vision.

Should I Just Accept the Fact That Men Are Selfish?

There is a big difference between a man who follows his true vision and a man distracted by his thoughts. When a man follows his vision he is whole and present. When a man is distracted in his thoughts, he is out of relationship and not present. He is heady and anxious. He feels slightly blocked in all kinds of ways: with money, creativity, sexuality, relationships, and so on.

You may notice that your man is distracted in his own selfish world. Don't accept that in your life. Don't think you have to go along with everything or anything he does. That's not the feminine gift at all.

Don't support your man's head trip. Support his deep vision and his true love. If he is confused and ambiguous, help him to rediscover and refocus his true vision.

Why Can't He Receive My Love?

Almost all men feel burdened by their intimate relationship. A man's reality consists of many activities and relationships. His relationship with you is one aspect of his reality. For you, the relationship may be at the core of your reality. For him, it is probably not. For most men, the core of their life is a mission of some kind. Their intimate relationship is a primary relationship, but not the core of their life.

You may call your man at work to tell him how much you love him. But if his mind is involved in business, your call interrupts his mission. You may say, "I just wanted to call and tell you I love you." He may feel, *Damn it! Why is she calling now? I'm so busy!* He may feel this even though you are loving him. Sometimes he will be able to receive your love, but often he will experience it as a distraction.

He may be abrupt with you, you feel hurt and let him know, and he wonders what you are complaining about, while you wonder why he can't feel your love.

In the daily practice of intimacy, your man has his responsibilities and you have yours. One of your responsibilities is to remember that his rejection of your interruption is not his rejection of *you*. He is rejecting an interference in his life. You can transcend what seems like an obvious rejection of you and realize that all he is doing is regretting being distracted from his work.

One of the biggest gifts you could give him is to develop your ability to feel, *Am I serving him in this moment? Is he benefiting from the way I am giving him love?* Or, *Am I being needy and clingy? Am I dramatizing my own neediness or am I relaxed in the knowledge of love?*

Are you bringing him true happiness when you talk to him? Are the emotions you bring to him serving his growth? If you feel you are serving his growth, then it doesn't matter what he says about it. Listen to what he says, and continue feeling in your heart, *Am I really serving him?* If you feel you are, then continue doing whatever serves him.

What Should I Do When He Ignores Me?

Imagine a moment when you are relaxed in love. You are not being needy or dramatizing your need for attention. You are offering your man a gift of love in your unique way—but he is not receiving it because he is absorbed in doing something else. In that moment, you could feel all of your possible responses: *Well, who needs him! Oh, I'm hurt. What am I doing wrong? I must not be doing enough. It must be my fault that he doesn't love me. Tough. If he doesn't like it that's his problem.*

We all respond differently when we do not feel loved. These responses are usually rooted in our childhood and early life experience. We can become aware of our habitual responses. Do we act like we don't need love? Do we retaliate and withdraw our love from him? Do we act like we are not hurt, but then punish him in some subtle way? Do we collapse or do we become rigid?

Assuming we all have a tendency to dramatize our feelings of rejection and anger, what is the best way to practice in a moment when we do not feel our love is being received by our partner?

Remain in love. Remain in as much of your own love-energy as possible. Relax in your heart and trust your own feminine reservoir of love.

As a child you may have felt rejected. Throughout your life you have built strategies to handle these feelings of rejection. As children, we learn not to express our fear, our hurt or our wounded heart. In our masculine-oriented society vulnerability is considered weak. Even as children, we quickly learn to hide our pain.

So, instead of remaining open in love even when your heart is wounded, you may do one of two things, depending on your habits from childhood. You may stay in your feminine energy, closing down, hiding in your shell and curling into your darkness. Or, you may learn to act tough and act masculine; especially when you are hurt by your partner. So when you feel rejected by your man, you may tend to shift from feminine openness to masculine toughness: "Listen to me!" Or, "I don't need you anyway."

When you feel rejected by your man, you may shift to your more masculine, more directive, more angular and pointed kind of energy. When this shift occurs, the distance between you and your man grows. His masculine is depolarized by your masculine energy. He begins treating you more like a man (fighting and debating with you) than as his chosen woman. So be aware if you shift to a more angular or sharp energy when he rejects you.

If, instead, you can relax into your feminine and stay open, even in the midst of pain, he will at least have the opportunity to feel you as a feminine, wounded lover, rather than as a sharp, masculine opponent. He will be able to feel your openness, your hurt, and embrace you as a man embraces his chosen woman, rather than butt heads like two masculine rams.

How Can I Get Him to Express His Real Emotions About Other Women?

You serve your man by helping him tune into his purpose, not by trying to get him to express his emotions. Emotions come and go. You best serve a man by helping him become more constant in his love and his purpose. You serve him by empowering his purpose, his direction and his love, not by obliging him to talk with you about his emotions.

When a man acts in a way that is really not in alignment with his true purpose, it feels dishonest to him. You serve him by helping him tune into his true heart's desire. Emotions change moment to moment, but the heart's desire is constant. Its direction may slowly change over time as it opens and matures, but it does not suddenly shift back and forth.

In terms of promiscuity, your man may feel horny. He might want to have sex with a woman he meets at the grocery store. So if you say to him, "Do whatever you feel," you would be empowering his promiscuity. Instead, you can serve his sensitivity by inviting him to consider, "Does having sex with her serve your highest purpose?"

When it comes to promiscuity, honesty and integrity, a good man will align his actions with his highest purpose or his heart truth—not with his emotions or his penis. Men often feel like having sex with all kinds of women. However, their heart-truth—if they are sensitive to it—may stop them from having sex because such action may not serve their highest purpose.

The future man, the evolved man, is a man willing to sacrifice everything else to live on the basis of his highest vision. His highest vision might mean his relationship, his creativity or his meditation. It might mean all kinds of things to different men, but ultimately it involves discovering and expressing the true self.

The true self is love itself. The true self is infinite love with no boundaries. This is who each of us is. When a man's life is guided by his true self, then his attractions to other women come and go but do not sway him. His commitment in love remains uncompromised.

A man feels whole only when he fully incarnates his highest vision, his highest purpose. When he lives on the basis of his highest purpose as consistently as possible he feels complete, and only then is he able to offer you his love without hesitation. As a woman in relationship with him, you could serve him best by continually reconnecting him to his highest purpose—rather than his momentary emotions—so he can express his true self, which is unbounded love. This may or may not have anything to do with talking about his emotions.

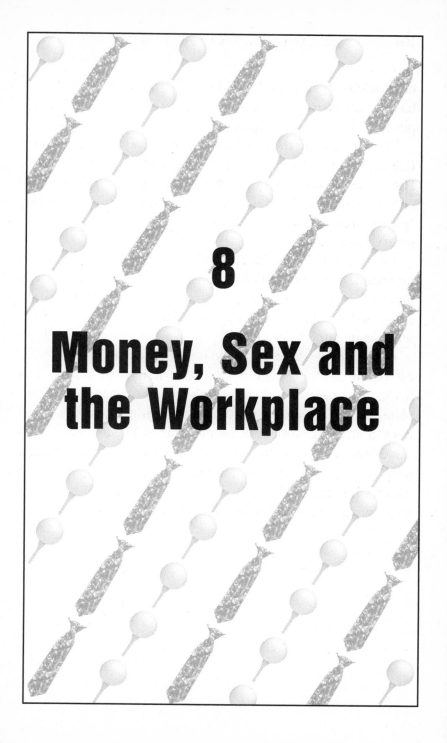

8

Money, Sex and the Workplace

Shouldn't Women Be Paid As Much As Men?

We still have a very patriarchal culture which denigrates and devalues the feminine. Our culture is changing slowly, but for many years everything that was considered good was a product of masculine energy. Today, people who are aggressively working their way to the "top" are still considered good and productive members of society. But if people are really enjoying each other, communing with nature, or obviously delighting in the sensual pleasures of the body, they aren't really looked upon as people who are contributing something valuable.

To make good money, we are expected to sacrifice our family life, our intimate life, even our personal health, while we push, push, push toward success. Most high-paying jobs in our culture entail an incredible amount of mental focus, organization and competition. Therefore, for both men and women, the masculine energy is more highly paid than the feminine.

It is not just men who are paid more, it is the masculine energy itself. Men and women are paid more for performing analytical and competitive masculine tasks than for feminine tasks, including anything involving a connection and sensitivity to the elements of nature, to true healing, to the preservation of life, and to loving, cooperative relationships.

Of course women and men should be paid the same amount of money if they do the same task. However, even deeper than a sex bias is the higher value our culture places on masculine, rather than feminine, styles of working, for both women and men. At this point of civilization's self-destructiveness, it may even be true that, temporarily, feminine tasks are more important than masculine tasks for our future on Earth. In any case,

in order for both men and women to be paid what they are
worth requires that our culture let go of its bias to overvalue
masculine energy.

Why Does His Financial Irresponsibility Bother Me So Much?

In our economically driven culture, when a man is weak in
his direction and vision, the first thing his woman will tend to
discuss with him is money. When a man isn't clear in his
vision, it's rare for his woman to say, "You are not clear in
your vision and I'm losing trust in you." Rather, she will tend
to say something like, "Do we have enough money for rent?
What have you been doing for the last month? I'm concerned
that we're not going to be able to pay our bills."

In our culture, money is an easy measure of a man's or
woman's masculine ability to guide his or her life and get
what he or she wants. Money reflects whether a man or
woman is able to cut through obstructions and achieve a goal,
at least in the world of commerce. Money is something you
can hold on to and count, whereas a subtle yet fundamental
distrust of your partner is more evasive. Usually when a
woman is disturbed about her man's way of dealing with
money, her feelings are actually a reflection of his lack of
purpose, his lack of deep, intuitive certainty of who he is, and
his inability to fully penetrate his woman's heart with love.

The cure for this is not necessarily to make more money.
Usually, the cure for a man is to really define his vision,
become clear about it, and live up to it on a daily basis. Then,
his woman will feel his masculine energy as it is liberated

from self-doubt. She feels his loving certainty expressed as commitment and full presence in relationship. She becomes certain of his love.

She usually doesn't need him to earn a specific number of dollars, although money may be part of the issue. She is not usually satisfied by his dollars as much as she is by his presence, his humor, his integrity and his depth of love for her.

In our culture, the demand for financial security is actually a demand for masculine energy, in a man or a woman. Because masculine skills are paid more than feminine skills, men and women must either cultivate their masculine or learn to get by with less money. When it comes to sexual polarity, money itself is not an issue. However, you will still find yourself depolarized when your partner is not paying his part of the bills. His lack of masculine integrity is a turn-off. The problem is not the lack of money itself, but your partner's lack of confident, clear and passionate masculine energy.

Why Do We Always Fight About Money?

If you are carrying the masculine energy in your intimacy, if you are supporting your man financially and arranging your living circumstance together, you will not be able to feel him as a *man*, unless he contributes strong masculine energy in another way. If he doesn't contribute strong masculine energy in some way, you will be able to relate to him as a housemate or even as a close friend, but, over time, you will lose your sexual polarization to him. His lack of masculine energy won't turn you on.

How can you trust him as your source of loving, masculine

force if he doesn't have it together enough to handle his life? You may still trust each other as friends, but you cannot fully trust each other as polarized lovers in committed intimacy if you are financially supporting him because he is not competent enough to do it.

It might be appropriate under certain conditions, of course, for a woman to support her man financially. Perhaps he is finishing work on a novel or a painting. Perhaps he is volunteering his time for important political or social causes. He might choose to serve humanity in a nonpaying position as a religious or visionary leader. Every situation is unique. There are many situations where a man could be full in his masculine energy, confident, passionate, and directed, and still be supported financially by his woman.

But if you don't trust your man because he is undirected, scattered, ambiguous or otherwise weak in his masculine energy, this will undercut your relationship, reducing your passion, your sexual attraction and your trust of each other.

A man feels his relationship with money is somewhat equivalent to his relationship with sexuality. If you are critical of his money-making abilities or career direction, even in the kindest way, it will turn him off. He will feel it in his body as if you were saying, "You are impotent and you don't satisfy me." He will feel it as a direct insult of his masculine force.

Have you noticed that usually when you talk about money with your man, he gets either weak or angry? It's really difficult to make suggestions in this area without causing a real scene.

In our culture, financial competence is frequently a good measure of masculine competence, though not always. It is understandable that a successful man is often a turn-on, and a man with weak masculine competence is often a turn-off. It is also understandable that discussing money with your man is as sensitive as discussing his skill, or lack of skill, as a lover.

Why Doesn't He Like to Talk About My Workday with Me?

If you are in your business mode day after day, it will probably depolarize your relationship. Even if you are good at business, your man will mostly experience your masculine energy—and men (masculine men, at least) are not polarized and attracted into intimacy by your masculine energy because they already possess masculine energy. It is your feminine love and energy that feel like gifts to them. The rest is just business. They could hire an accountant or a business associate to work with them on the finances. But nobody can hire a goddess.

If you are talking business all the time, it is like your man running away from cockroaches or sitting around listlessly watching TV all the time. You are each failing to live your sexual essence fully.

When he loves you, when his life is clear, directional and motivated for the highest good, he is full in his sexual essence and you are polarized by his masculine energy. You can trust him. You can relax as a woman and feel his masculine love deep in your heart. You feel his full presence. He is sensitive to your needs. You can feel his integrity, humor and happiness.

Likewise, he is polarized by your feminine love which opens his heart and gives him life. He may appreciate your business acumen just as you may appreciate his taste in clothing. But if his taste in clothing ruled his life, or your business activity ruled yours, you would not feel polarized toward each other. Your passion for one another would decrease and conflict would increase.

It is fine, of course, for you to be highly successful, creative and powerful in the business world. We should each learn to give our natural gifts, whatever they are. However, in addition to being successful, if you want a man who will ravish you in love, day after day, who will always be there for you, who will penetrate your heart with his loving no matter what your mood, then you must reciprocate his trustable masculine energy with your trustable feminine. Regardless of your financial success, in polarized intimacy you must be free as a goddess, connected to your heart, wild, gifting with love, dancing without inhibition in the light and the dark.

Your masculine force may be a key to your financial success in our culture, but your feminine force is a key to fulfilling reciprocation in the emotional dance of sexually polarized intimates.

What If I Am Better at Handling Our Finances Than He Is?

Is it more important to do things your way rather than his way, or is it more important to magnify sexually transmitted love in your relationship? This is a moment-by-moment decision. It might take your man an extra 10 minutes to figure something out without your help, but in exchange for those 10 minutes you may enhance emotional and sexual polarity by empowering his masculine energy. It is up to you to decide if the trade-off is worth it.

For many couples, the woman is better at financial matters than her man. She is better at making financial decisions, budgeting and investing their money.

Arranging the finances involves masculine energy: organizing, planning, projecting, disciplining spending behavior and setting and reaching goals. If the woman takes financial responsibility for the couple, it will tend to depolarize the relationship—unless it is done very artfully.

One way to handle the finances with minimum conflict is to set aside a certain time and place in which you function as business partners rather than as intimate partners. You might say, "For the next hour, let's go to the kitchen table and do finances." For this hour, your man isn't going to experience you as his woman, in particular. He will experience you as a financial planner. He may argue with you or be bored with you. This switch needs to be all right with you. For this hour, he isn't going to treat you as his woman, as his wife or as his lover, but as a financial consultant.

Then, after an hour, clearly switch out of your role as financial consultant. Perhaps you take a shower and change clothes to help you shift the energy. When you come back together as intimate partners don't bring up the finances again until your next meeting, if at all possible. Handle the finances completely during the appointed hour, or however long it takes. This is one way for you to handle the finances without unintentionally depolarizing the relationship.

Another way is to arrange the finances without projecting masculine energy toward your man. Just sit down with the books and take care of business. Don't involve him. Because you do it yourself, he doesn't experience your masculine energy. He knows you are taking care of it. He appreciates that you are better at it than he is. But he doesn't experience your masculine energy face to face. Whoever handles the finances, and how they are handled, are crucial factors in the presence or lack of sexual polarity in intimacy.

Why Are Men Often Hostile Toward Professional Women?

In our day-to-day lives, especially in our "modern" culture, both men and women must be highly developed in their masculine energy in order to survive economically. Unfortunately, a woman in her masculine energy at the workplace should expect men to treat her somewhat like a man, which might mean swearing or verbally pushing her around, as men do with each other as friends. Men make blunt comments with each other fairly frequently. A man might be with his best friend and say, "Don't be an idiot. That's the stupidest thing I've ever heard."

One aspect of the masculine form of communication is the assumption of mutual warriorship, involving the challenge of self and other. If you don't mind being treated this way, like one of his male counterparts, then it's fine to project masculine energy. You will be treated like a fellow warrior— although some men may become confused by a woman warrior.

It's difficult for some men to deal with you if, at your core, you are very feminine, yet you are being very masculine to get a job done. These men feel your naturally attractive feminine energy and also feel the sword of the masculine from you. A man must shut off his sensitivity to your feminine energy if he is to relate to you as a business associate rather than as a source of feminine energy.

It is only recently that women have been expected to act like men do. Before this period of history, for both good and bad reasons, men and women often had separate domains of work. This division eventually became a role that each sex was put into and then was expected to perform in accordance with rigid stereotypes. This role typing is entirely negative; men and women should have equal access to everything. They are free to be any way they want.

In the last 30 or so years women have excelled in high-paying professions that were previously the domain of men. But this kind of work does have its consequences on intimate relationships: It's hard to let go of your accumulated masculine energy at the end of a workday.

Imagine that all day you are in the fast world of business. You make quick decisions and tell people what to do. Come six o'clock it's hard to flip a switch and be a radiant goddess, a deeply relaxed woman. It's not so easy to let go of a day's worth of masculine energy. This is one major cause of the deadening of sexual polarity between intimate partners who both work at jobs that require masculine energy.

Does Working with Women Ruin My Man?

Imagine a man who spends the whole day at work treating women as sexually neutral associates. At the end of the day he comes home to his woman. He has just spent eight hours closing off his sexuality and the flow of his emotional-sexual feelings. When he comes home to you he is not very sensitive. He is rather closed and weary.

At work, most men are sexually attracted to many women every day. The way a man often responds to feminine energy is with sexual interest. It is not a mental choice so much as an innate, bodily polarization. Women experience this polarization too, but it is not necessarily so directional or sexual.

Imagine you are sitting and talking with a group of women friends and a really handsome, powerful man walks into the room. Your energy, as a woman, shifts. The way you hold yourself shifts. Your breath may even shift in response to the masculine energy.

Men have a similar response to the feminine, but their response often includes sexual attraction. When men are together with other men, a lot of what they talk about is women—their bodies, their sexiness and their attractiveness. Most men don't act on their frequent sexual desires. Instead, most men confine their sexual activity to their chosen partner. However, a large percentage of a man's sexual life is spent fantasizing about having sex with other women.

As a woman, you probably don't experience a struggle within yourself because you want to go to bed with dozens of men you see every day. Some women would, but not most. However, most men are. It might be difficult for you to find this out, because very few men will admit it to a woman. However, most men are rather polygamous, at least in their secret desires.

Most men spend part of their day at the workplace suppressing their sexuality, suppressing their feelings of attraction, and suppressing their native masculine response to the feminine energy of the women they work with. When your man comes home to you it's hard for him to sweep you off your feet and tell you how much he loves you. He has spent his whole day shutting down his response to the feminine. He has turned himself off to the feminine.

So, even though it's positive socially, politically and economically for men and women to have equal access to all positions, it has served to undermine our intimate emotional and sexual lives. How much of your workday involves subtle flirtation or innuendo? Sexual energy is almost constantly being transmitted between men and women at a subtle level. All of this was avoided in more traditional settings where men and women had their own separate cultures. But today is a different time and we are learning a new way to live.

When Discussing Business, Why Do Men Like to Exclude Women?

Men are actually not as good at being businessmen when women are around them. For one thing, when men are in their masculine energy and are with a woman, they often feel sexual energy toward her. Their masculine and feminine energies create a natural arc of polarity.

So, if men don't want to be sexually distracted by their women co-workers, they have to cut back their masculine energy. But when they cut back their masculine energy, they also cut back on their decision-making capacity, their aggressiveness and their ability to focus.

There is another aspect to it. When several men are around a woman, they compete for her. It happens automatically at the biological level. Not only are the men in the room working on a deal, they are trying to look good in front of the woman.

For these reasons and more, many men don't like women around when they are doing business. Men may not fully understand the dynamic of sexual polarity, yet they feel it. They don't admit, "Well, I compete with other men when she's around so I'd rather she be out of the room." Instead, men say to one another in exasperation, "Women!" They can't admit the sexual dynamic, yet it is obvious to most men.

Polarity is a real force. It is something to be honored. The presence of feminine energy changes masculine energy. Men and women must respect the force of sexual polarity and find creative means to work together. They need to understand each other's natural sexual response without being judgmental about their differences. Sexual polarity is a big factor in the workplace, whether we like it or not.

How Serious Are Men's Sexual Fantasies About Their Female Co-Workers?

Most men are sexually attracted to many different women every day. If you ask them, "How many times a day are you sexually attracted to women?" they might honestly answer, "How many women do I see?" A good portion of their day involves being sexually attracted to women, although they don't usually act on it.

When men see an attractive woman, they don't necessarily feel an emotional desire for relationship. It's more like the desire for an ice cream sundae, for a moment of delicious pleasure. It doesn't necessarily have any emotional depth to it. They are not thinking about leaving their wives every time they see another woman. It's a momentary biological desire.

So if you are an attractive woman in the workplace, the men are going to be sitting there fantasizing about sex with you. You may wonder, "What the hell is going on here?" You are just trying to do your job.

But there is also another side to this play of attraction. If you are going to your workplace wearing makeup, dressing attractively, aware of your sexiness, then you are expecting to be seen as a woman. You are not shaving your head and going to work in a gray sack or something like a nun's outfit. If you were, then you might be able to avoid this whole dynamic. Or maybe not—men at work might still be polarized to your sheer sexual energy, with no embellishment at all.

The way men experience your attractiveness is as sexual desire in their bodies. So they think you must feel the same sense of desire in your body, "She's open to sex." Of course, you may not be feeling this way at all. But that's their natural bodily response to your natural feminine energy.

All of their lives, men learn how to cut off their sexual desire so they don't get into trouble. When men get together, though, they can relax and let it out. They talk about the women they have seen and want. Men know how meaningless it is. They may say, "Did you see Betsy? I'd really like to have her!" They don't think about the whole issue or feel the emotional depths of it. It's more like, "I'd sure like some chocolate ice cream!" The other guy says, "I'd like some strawberry ice cream." Then it's back to work. There's no depth to it at all.

Should I Support Myself Even If He Wants to Support Me?

For many men, meeting the challenge in the marketplace or elsewhere is itself rewarding. It might be the struggle of surfing a wave, writing a novel, struggling with inner demons through meditation or with opponents through martial arts. But it is the struggle itself, the battle, that many men really enjoy.

Although women also enjoy money, success and becoming full in their art or profession, they don't necessarily enjoy the sheer struggle of it: getting out there and competing with others, seeing who's better, and making it happen against all odds. This competitive struggle isn't as attractive for most women as it is for most men.

Men love battles, struggles and competition. If they aren't living it in their lives they get it through football games on TV, combat movies, financial gambles, spiritual searches, arguing philosophy and politics or creating a war. But most women are not as interested in these things as men.

To honor each other's uniqueness as woman and man we need to go through a period of learning that it's not about who "should" do what. If I'm afraid of cockroaches, it's not something that I should be embarrassed about. If my woman is heavily involved in playing high-stakes poker games, fine.

Your man may be moved to cherish you and protect you in a certain way, not because you are weak, but because you are radiant, precious and beautiful to him. He knows that when you have to go out and compete in the masculine-dominated business world, you will have to dampen your radiance and take up the sword, to some extent. He may want to relieve you of this obligation. On the other hand, you might really enjoy and excel at business. It's an individual matter. You and your man will have to learn your unique ways of gifting each other.

You may be equally happy and able to take up the sword and compete in the world of hardball business as you are able to be fully relaxed, radiant and open in love and sensual ecstasy.

But the fact is, as a culture, we have denied the feminine, and many women live a life compromised by masculine economic pressures in a masculine business world. Taking on so much masculine energy stresses their body, breath and emotions. They experience a sense of emptiness and anxiety. Due to holding excess masculine energy in their bodies, and protecting or hiding their feminine energy by neuromuscularly "armoring" themselves, many women may eventually experience symptoms of physical disease, especially in the more feminine parts of their body.

We deny the feeling of sweet surrender. We suppress the ecstasy of the heart. For whatever reason, the momentum of the world has led to the masculine force being more accepted than the feminine. The masculine is considered productive and efficient, but it's not necessarily the most fulfilling. We can make the happiest choice of both, the way of the sword and the way of the goddess, once we know the value of both and can experience both without stress. The warrior can gift the goddess, and the goddess can gift the warrior, whether we are talking about the warrior and the goddess inside each of us or the unique gifts shared between partners.

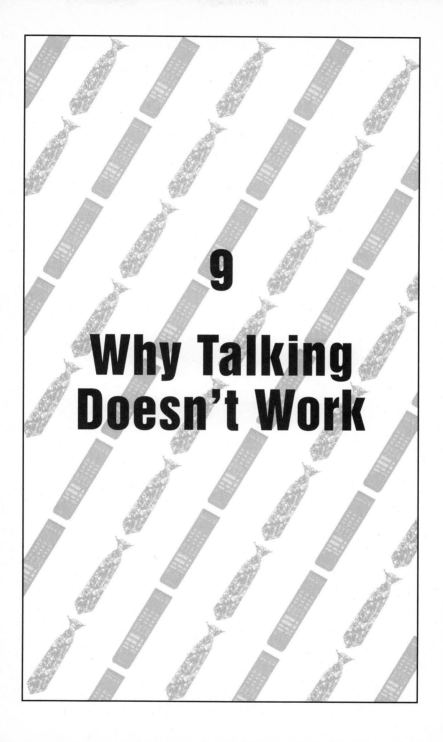

9

Why Talking Doesn't Work

How Do I Create Intimacy?

You create intimacy moment by moment. You set the level of intimacy in a relationship by how much you reveal yourself. If you repress feelings when your man is talking, he will probably do the same.

You will either attract a man who is as equally open to intimacy as you are, or you will set up a resonance field which will induce your man to be as open as you. You can't expect complete intimacy on his part if you're hesitant to let him know what's really going on inside of you.

Why Can't We Communicate?

Many difficulties in relationships occur because people assume that men and women are pretty much the same. And they are similar from certain perspectives. Both men and women have two arms and two legs for instance. At the spiritual level men and women are also identical. That is, they are identical at the level of light, the level of unconditional love. But just about everything between the level of molecules and unconditional love is different between men and women.

One of the differences between men and women is in the way they talk.

We each have three "centers" of communication in our body. The doing or action center is located near the navel. The emotional or feeling center is located in the chest. The thinking center is located in the head.

Most men speak from either their navel, the doing center, or from their head, the thinking center. When a man is listening to you, he hears whatever you say through these two centers. When you talk with a man and you say something like, "I don't feel great today," he will probably say something like, "What do you want to do?" He will try to solve the problem for you; tell him a feeling and he will respond with an action. Either that, or he'll start analyzing you: "I think your feelings are due to your parents." Or, "When does your period start?"

You might ask, "How are you feeling about Joe?" Your man might answer, "I want to kill the guy," rather than saying, "I'm feeling angry." He won't describe his emotions. He will describe his desire for action.

Most women, by contrast, tend to speak and listen from their emotional center, from their chest area. For instance, when he asks what you want to *do* about something, you tend to describe your *feelings*. You say, "I'm losing my job." He says, "What are you going to do?" And you answer, "I'm feeling scared."

Between intimate partners, the conversation can also go something like this:

He: "Do you want to go to the Smiths tonight?"

She: "Well, last time I saw Judy Smith she made me feel really uncomfortable."

He: "Okay, but do you want to go to see them tonight?"

She: "Well, what do *you* feel like doing?"

He: "I feel like I want to know what we're going to do tonight."

He gets frustrated because you don't communicate in terms of action and analysis. You get frustrated and feel, *Where's the connection between us?* By understanding these natural differences between men and women, we can avoid a lot of conflict.

You can actually practice speaking from any of the three

centers. You can learn to speak in *doing* words, *feeling* words or *thought* words. If you really want to resonate with your man, for instance, take a moment and translate your feelings into action sentences. Then he will get it right away.

This is a tiny difference that makes all the difference.

How Can I Talk So He Understands Me?

One method for full communication is to tell your partner what you *think, feel* and *want* to do. For instance, you could say, "When you tell me how to fix the toilet, I *think* you consider me stupid, I *feel* hurt and I *want* to hit you with this wrench." You express all three: thoughts, feelings and desires.

You could use this form of communication when he isn't making money. "When you sit in front of the TV instead of doing business, I think you're irresponsible, I feel abandoned and I want to trust you."

It's always good to communicate to your partner how his actions affect you. By speaking in terms of thinking, feeling and wanting, he has a much better chance of connecting with you and understanding you.

Why Does He Think I'm Stupid?

Men are essentially problem solvers. They want a problem to solve. They see everything as a problem to solve, even your emotions. When you tell him how you feel, a man will immediately try to figure out ways to "solve" your feeling.

This is their masculine energy at work.

Telling somebody what to do, how to solve a problem, is an expression of masculine energy. When your man tells you what to do, for instance, it is not a judgment that you don't know what to do. He would tell anyone what to do.

This is a classic confusion between men and women. Women often feel, "If he is telling me what to do he must assume that I'm incompetent." Many men tell people what to do regardless of who they tell and what that person knows. The more masculine a man is, the more he tells everybody what to do. It is not based on an assumption that nobody knows what to do. It is just an expression of masculine energy. How many times has your man told you what to do when it was obvious you knew what to do? Probably many times. Your man isn't necessarily operating from an assumption that you don't know what to do. He is merely expressing his masculine energy.

Why Does He Criticize My Emotionality?

From his perspective, a man wonders, "Why do women give so much credence to their emotions? They change so fast. They come and go." So, in general, men want women to de-emphasize emotionality. Women, on the other hand, want men to communicate with more emotionality. However they communicate, men and women are both learning to love.

Love is not necessarily rational nor is it necessarily emotional. Love is granted with no expectations. It is a gift, a blessing. It is more true of us than the beating of our hearts, whereas emotions and thoughts come and go. When we are relaxed and happy, love is who we are. Emotions and thoughts, however, are always changing.

Some women feel that emotions are more real than analysis. Some men think analysis is more important than emotions. Yet people who are not wildly emotional can be totally in love. People who are not great thinkers can be totally in love. Love can be real regardless of our mental or emotional state.

Is He Blind to How I'm Feeling?

Men usually need to hear about your feelings in words. For them to really understand you, you usually have to say something like, "I'm feeling hurt." If you indicate your feelings with a subtle posture change or a pregnant silence, your man will just wonder what's happening—or not even notice. Because your man is probably not as sensitive to your emotions as you are to his, he'll need verbal capsulizations of what you are feeling.

Perhaps you are not able to put your feelings into words. You might just say, "There is something going on." But even this is better then expecting him to sense something is going on. Most men really need some kind of verbal description, even something as simple as, "Something is happening and I can't describe it." This is far better than expecting him to sense something in you or read your mind.

The best you can do is to actually describe your emotions to him. For instance, "I'm feeling hurt." He'll probably be surprised, "Why are you hurt?" You may say, "I'm in love with you, so when you pull away from me toward your business,

I want to let you know how it affects me, even though you may need to do business." At least you will expand his awareness of how his life affects you.

It helps for each of you to expand each other's awareness. His actions unknowingly affect you and your actions unknowingly affect him. Let him know how you are affected rather than keeping your emotions unspoken, expecting him to sense what you are feeling.

Men love to work through things. They love to solve things. So talk to him in a way that invites his action. "When you abruptly turn away to work I feel hurt. Maybe there is something we can do about this."

Then he thinks, "Maybe there is something we can do about it." He won't assume a barrier between you. It will be something to work out, and that will be fine with him. But if he turns away from you to do some business and you begin to cry, he'll be at a total loss. He needs your verbal communication.

You need to communicate your feelings in a way that he can understand, rather than expect him to sense what's going on with you. Men rarely sense exactly what's going on with you. A day or two later they may say, "Is something going on?" But by then you're purple in the face.

What Should I Do When I'm Unable to Speak?

Put your feelings in verbal form, at least silently to yourself. Label them. "This is anger." "This is sorrow." "I feel hurt." Do this every time you notice you are feeling something, especially in response to what he is doing. Learn to put verbal labels on your feelings and eventually you will be able to say them out loud. Your man needs your words, especially at first. Eventually, words may not be so necessary, but in the meantime, words are a bridge that will help you communicate your feelings to your man.

Are All Men Dishonest?

When you sense that your man is not being honest, instead of asking him to get in touch with his emotions, ask him what his purpose is. To be honest, a man needs to be aligned with his purpose rather than his emotions.

For a woman to be honest, she must contact her emotions. She feels what is inside of her and expresses her true feelings. For a woman, this is honesty. But for a man, honesty is aligning himself to his highest vision, his vision of the Divine, or truth—not to his emotions of the moment. You might ask him, "What are you going toward? What is your highest purpose?" He must examine whether his actions and words are supporting his purpose. If they are not supporting his highest purpose, then he is being dishonest.

Most men don't have the ability to regulate their honesty with their emotions. For men, emotions are not honesty; emotions change all the time. For men, what is honest is alignment with purpose.

For a man, the distance between his words and his purpose is the error measure of his honesty. To a man, honesty means aligning his words and actions with his purpose. This is why men are sometimes so poker-faced. At times, their integrity might mean *not* saying something in order to accomplish the highest purpose. This, to him, is the most honest thing to do.

At some point in your relationship, you will probably catch your man telling a lie. Try to remember that, just as most women will say anything when moved by their strong emotions, most men will say anything when moved by their highest purpose. To most women, a strong emotion justifies saying all kinds of things that might not be entirely true in the big picture. They are simply emotional expressions in the moment.

Likewise, to most men, a strong purpose justifies saying things that may not be entirely true in the big picture. Honesty usually means something different to men and women.

Why Can't He Listen to My Suggestions?

Imagine a situation where the man is not as interested in sex as his woman. He seems neutralized, uninterested. So, she may become more and more aggressive. She may make stronger sexual advances toward him. She may suggest they see a therapist or go to a relationship workshop. Perhaps she tries to talk to him about it, hoping he will become motivated to do something.

The more she wants to direct the relationship, the less sexually interested he will become. Many times, for instance, the woman will say, "Let's go to a relationship workshop," and the man will say, "No." The reason for his refusal is simple: He can't go to the workshop and also carry the masculine energy in the relationship unless he has directed himself to the workshop.

While the masculine way is directive, the feminine way is attractive. The feminine way is to open doorways. Whether or not the man enters the doorway must be entirely his decision if he is going to carry the masculine energy in relationship. To open the doorway a woman might say, "I heard about a workshop that I'm very excited about." This feels very different to a man than saying, "Let's go to this workshop." One is an open door. The other is a suggested direction. It might seem strange, but the effect each of these statements has on a man is very different.

Shouldn't I Be Able to Say Anything I Want to My Man?

There is an art to communication which involves understanding what the listener is capable of hearing. For example, you do not talk about the intimate details of your sex life with your five-year-old daughter. It is not appropriate. You do not tell your grandmother all about your more unconventional exploits because she probably wouldn't understand. It wouldn't serve anything.

In the same way, telling your man what to do is sometimes not appropriate if your intention is to maintain sexual polarization and attraction. There are certain times, of course, when you need to tell him very directly what to do, but these occasions are relatively rare between two individuals who are polarized and sensitive to each other's needs.

There is a way to communicate directly with your man while relaxing in your feminine energy and empowering his masculine energy. By doing this your intimacy remains sexually polarized. When he receives this type of communication, he embraces you as his chosen woman instead of getting into competition with you, which is what he would do in relation to your masculine energy.

How do you change your man's behavior without using your masculine energy to tell him what to do? Tell him your feeling. Try saying, "I'm cold" instead of saying, "Please chop wood for the fire." Try saying, "I'm tired," instead of telling him, "Let's go home now." Try saying, "I'm getting nervous," instead of saying, "Don't make this business deal." Open a doorway with your feelings. By letting him generate his own course of action, you allow him to carry the masculine energy and he remains sexually polarized to you, masculine to feminine.

If complete communication is more important to you than sexual polarization, use all three modes of communication as described earlier: thinking, feeling and doing. However, if you want to maximize polarity, then tell him how you feel rather than what you want him to do. Your feminine energy will be felt as an invitation, whereas your masculine energy may be faced as a challenge.

If He Isn't Interested in Talking About My Day, What Should I Do?

Sharing the details of your day is a way to share love in a friendship. But try to notice if your man is really interested in hearing about your day, if such talk draws him nearer to you in love. Notice if such talk enlivens him and makes him happy, or if it depolarizes him.

For instance, men with strong masculine purpose rarely want to exchange chitchat with you about your day. Such chitchat serves only to distance them. Instead, be fully present with him. Invite his presence. Engage love directly, physically, spiritually and emotionally. Allow your verbal mind to rest for a few moments, and drink deeply of love together. Look into each other's eyes. Hold each other. Praise each other. Use language only as a way to give love.

Talk about the details of your day with your women friends. They will enjoy your sharing and resonate with your concerns and emotions.

The practice of an intimate love relationship is not merely a friendship. It is a partnership that operates at a different wavelength than friendship. In your intimate relationship, notice what kind of talk serves to magnify love.

Sometimes, no talking at all is the best way to communicate love. For a few days, try spending an hour each day being present with your man without either one of you talking at all. Communicate love to each other without saying a word. Touch each other. Gaze at each other. Allow love to be transmitted through sexual embrace, if this feels natural. During this hour, whatever you do, try transmitting love to one another without any words at all.

In our verbally based modern life, we often think talking is the best way to communicate love with our intimate partner. Sometimes it is and sometimes it isn't. Feel the effects of your words on each other. If your words transmit love, fine. If you feel him or yourself becoming turned off by each other's words, relax, breathe, and reconnect with the love in your heart. Explore other ways to transmit love. Through experimentation, find what works best for you. And in the meantime, spend plenty of time with close friends who can truly empathize and enjoy sharing the details of the day with you.

Why Does He Cut Me Short and Interrupt Me, Even When I'm Loving Him?

The masculine and the feminine communicate love very differently, but few of us understand these differences. We don't have very good models in our society for the strong masculine or the strong feminine. Most people are learning to get beyond the stage in which the feminine craves to be loved and gives up her own authority in order to get love, and the masculine craves money and power and gives up his authentic center in this pursuit.

A masculine character who is connected to his center, to his heart, is like a samurai warrior of love. He is a man who cuts through all bullshit. He doesn't tolerate any bullshit, but he is not macho, wanting position and admiration. Rather, he slices through bullshit with humor and reveals love.

Masculine love has a cutting-through quality, yet it is also deeply caring. In an evolved man, the forceful quality isn't used to hurt or downgrade anyone. It is used to open the way for more love. If you or your man are talking about something that does not contribute to love, he may say, "I don't want to continue this way. I love you."

The way the feminine communicates love isn't so much by "getting to the point" as it is by taking time to share feelings. It is like the way many women shop, flowing through the aisles of goods on display, rather than darting in, getting what is needed, and darting out. The masculine darts straight to the purpose, "Here is the point. What is your answer?" Men often ask of their women, "What's your point? What are you trying to get at?" He does not realize that the flow of communication, your sharing of feelings, *is* the message of love.

Because men and women communicate differently, your man may find it difficult to follow the way you talk. The feminine talks more like a river than like a freight train, flowing in twists and turns rather than charging in a straight line to some final destination. If your man doesn't understand this, he may interrupt you or cut you short. He wants you to communicate like he does, which is less about sharing and more about reaching a conclusion.

What Should I Do If My Man Keeps Talking Business and I Want to Play?

If you don't want to talk business, then don't. If he starts talking about business, you could say, "I really like the way you smile." If he says the commodity market has been taking a downturn lately, you could say, "The sound of your voice is really nice." Your words bring him back to the realm of the senses, the realm of energy, which is where you want to relax into.

He will experience this as a gift. He has men friends that he could talk shop with; you can be the goddess who invites him out of his mental world, into his body, and into relationship with you.

Do this by staying in the energy which you prefer: "I want to go to dinner with this man. I don't want to talk shop. I want to have fun." He may be sitting there at the dinner table barking out stock market quotes, and you could say, "This tastes so good. Did you taste this? Taste a bite of this." Bring him back into the realm of the senses.

Essentially, welcome him back into the garden of the feminine. He is up in the sky talking about concepts. Welcome him down into the fragrant garden, into the world of life. You can do this very concretely and literally. "Taste this delicious salad." You could say, "I love the way the skin crinkles around your eyes." Bring him back into the world of love, the world of the body.

The more you relax into your body and your senses, the more you will polarize and attract him. You might not always want to do this, of course. You could talk about business whenever you want. But be aware that what attracts him as a man to you as a woman is your ability to welcome him into the world of life, rather than the world of verbal debate, mental concepts and future goals.

To get what you want, relax and play. This will also give him what he wants in a woman, which is the feminine force, the goddess. A masculine man will choose to be with you intimately because your feminine energy balances and heals him deeply, and his heart will naturally open to your feminine love.

Your man might talk business because he is on automatic pilot; because he is unaware. He may be treating you like a business colleague instead of like a lover. Your gift of feminine energy will remind him to let go of his mental concerns and relax with you in the bodily play of smiling lovers.

Why Do Our Conversations Feel So Empty?

Most of the talk that men do with men is about doing: working, business, projects. If a woman gets carried into this instead of being relaxed in her own strength, then the relationship becomes one-sidedly masculine. The feminine part of her feels unsatisfied. She is not getting what she wants.

Sometimes it happens the other way. The woman starts talking about her emotions and her needs, which are very different from her man's. So the man relinquishes his natural domain and enters into her world of foreign moods. Then he feels unsatisfied. He has no real interest in the sharing of these kinds of emotions.

Men are often limited in their spectrum of emotional response; women are often quite wide in it. Don't expect him to always participate with you. Continue to trust in your feelings. Always relax into exactly what you are in any particular moment.

Your desire for your man to enter into your world of feelings and emotions is like his desire for you to enter into his world of theory and projects. These desires are fine, temporarily. But if the relationship tends to go toward one or the other most of the time it becomes one-sided. One person will begin to feel unsatisfied and unfulfilled in the relationship.

You will feel unfulfilled if you talk mostly about theory and business with him. He will feel unfulfilled if you talk mostly about feelings and emotions. You will be gifting each other if you invite each other into the present, not into his head or your emotions, which are both filled with residue from the past. Find a way for both of you to share love in the present without any emotional or mental reference to the past.

How Can I Change My Man's Ways?

When you take off the limitations on what men do together it sometimes gets rowdy. If you look at traditional men's activities they are often forms of competition, debate, challenge, even death. Sports, hunting, boxing and war are essentially men's clubs. Men love war. Men might not love killing people, but they love war, the game of war: opponents, competition, the risk of death. Men love that. Most sports are a ritualized form of war. Something is at stake. The challenge is on.

If you want to debate and compete with your man, offer him a challenge. Confront him with masculine energy. Tell him what to do. If you don't want to do battle with him, then have one of his men friends tell him what to do. This is a form of wisdom that still operates in traditional communities: Men straighten each other out. More often than not, if a woman tries to change her man's direction he will get angry and will not change. Let another man bring it to him. Let them do battle. Let them get to the bottom of it. This is one way men exchange love with one another.

If He Can Tell Me What to Do, Why Can't I Tell Him What to Do?

Imagine you are making love and you say to your man, "You don't know how to make love. Your penis doesn't work very well." Your comment, however truthful, isn't going to sexually excite him. In fact, it will probably turn him off, immediately—instant depolarization.

An essential masculine quality is directionality. Any time a woman is critical of her man's directionality he receives it as a criticism of his essential masculine energy. It is equivalent to you telling him that he is a lousy lover. It is equivalent not merely because he has a delicate ego, but because you are criticizing his directionality, the quality which is closest to his identity as a man.

If a man says that you are ugly and smell bad, are you hurt merely because you have a delicate ego? It is a criticism of your essential radiance, your natural feminine attractiveness. Such a criticism will depolarize you immediately, regardless of whether it is true or not.

It is the same for a man. Any time a woman says something to her man which implies that his decision or direction is not good, he feels she is saying, "You are not a true man." If in some way you tell your man he should be doing something differently, if your attitude says, "You are not doing it right," he will feel it as a criticism of his essential masculinity and he will be depolarized.

If you want to avoid depolarization, then tell your man how you *feel* rather than criticize what he is *doing*. For instance, if you are making love and you are uncomfortable, instead of saying, "You can't make love very well," you might say, "I'm hurting." Or, you might just move your body a little bit, changing your position.

It's the same way in all aspects of your relationship. You might know your man is on the wrong track. Sometimes it is appropriate to simply say, "You're on the wrong track." For instance, it may not be a moment in which you are hoping for polarity or attraction between you and him. But if you want to put him on the right track *without* depolarizing him, try saying, "I'm uncomfortable." If he tells you his plans and they make you anxious, say, "I'm feeling anxious," rather than, "That's ridiculous."

If you say, "I'm feeling anxious," you are inviting him to change without giving him masculine energy. You are guiding him and directing him through the invitation of your feminine energy. You are teaching him to discover a better direction, and you both remain polarized through the process. If it is not your priority to be polarized, then you could say anything you want.

Not all couples want polarized relationships. Some couples are involved in a marriage of convenience or a relationship based on mutual business interests. Some couples concentrate on being parents, or friends, more than on being lovers. Each couple is unique, and polarity may be more or less important to them. But if you want to give and receive sexually transmitted love, then polarity is essential.

How Can I Get My Man to Make a Decision Without Creating Tension?

Imagine that you and your man are supposed to visit some friends for the evening. He's just come home from working all day. He's been wielding his masculine sword all day long and he's tired and ready to put it down. He flops onto the sofa and wants to relax. He doesn't want to make any more decisions. But you realize that in order to get to your friend's house on time, some decisions need to be made and some things need to be taken care of before you leave. You need to get ready soon or you'll be late.

You could come into the room and tell your man, "It's getting late. We have to make some decisions and get going."

If you did so, you would be using masculine energy. He would probably experience this as nagging. You might be very loving, but because his masculine energy is weary, your strong directionality will feel very masculine, as though you're bossing him around.

There is a key to making this kind of situation work: If you could be more feminine than he is, he will experience himself as masculine, regardless of how weary he is. Therefore, he will take responsibility to make a decision.

How do you empower his masculine so he makes a decision? Imagine he is laying on the couch, finally relaxing after a day of work. He doesn't want to make any decisions. You're thinking, "We have 10 minutes to make some decisions and act." So, you sit down next to him, snuggle up against him, and put your head on his lap. He'll immediately begin to feel masculine compared to you.

You may say, "We are supposed to be at the Smith's at seven o'clock, but I'll just stay here all night with you if you want." He'll feel, *Someone has to make a decision here.* By consciously being more feminine than he is, you make him aware of his masculine energy. You put the ball in his court. Now, he carries the masculine energy, whereas if you came in and demanded that he make a decision, you would be carrying the masculine energy. If this doesn't work, then just make a decision for yourself. But at least you've given him the opportunity to direct with *his* masculine and maintain polarity.

This is a conscious way to wield energy in relationship so you remain polarized with one another. It is not a matter of secret manipulation. It is a way to communicate that allows the force of polarized love to remain strong between you. It is not deception. He knows what you are doing. You know what he is doing. He would probably prefer you to be this way, polarizing his masculine energy with your feminine. You may want to ask your man which style of communication he would prefer you used.

10

How to Prepare a Man for Intimacy

Are All Men Obsessed with Something Other Than Intimacy?

The priority for the feminine energy in all of us is love. The priority for the masculine energy in all of us is freedom. Therefore, when a man is in his masculine energy his priority is freedom. What freedom means to a man is enlightenment, ultimately, and being free to act on the basis of his highest vision, to act on the basis of what is most meaningful to him.

If the most meaningful thing you could do is write a novel, to be free in your masculine means that you write it. It means that you go through and beyond your own laziness. You battle your own inner demons. You battle the external world if you need to. If you need to somehow make money so you can write, you do it. You arrange your relationships so you can write. And you actually write, you actually do it. For a man, or anyone in their masculine, freedom involves all of this.

To another man, living his freedom might mean meditating, or making money, or perfecting his game of golf. It is different for each man. But for any man to be living on the basis of his freedom, he must be actually involved in the moment-to-moment fruition of his deepest desire and the unfolding of his highest vision.

When he does that, he is also free to love a woman, to love you. But when the freedom or purpose of a man's life isn't being lived fully, then his love gets withdrawn in confusion and weakness. In order to fully love a woman, a man must be living his life on the basis of his true vision.

Does He Really Want to Leave Me or Is It Just a Phase?

As a woman you have an innate sense of what love is. You can sense the incredible reservoir of love that you are. You can feel the love inside you and you look for a way to give it or to share it.

Sure, there might be barriers to your loving. There might be childhood resistances that temporarily limit your expression of love. There might be all kinds of things that cover up your love. But, as a woman, you have an innate sense of love and your ability to give and receive love.

Most men don't. The innate knowledge of your man is probably not about love, but about his destiny, his purpose. Yet, there may be a lot covering up his sense of true purpose as well, and it usually has to do with fear. Frequently, a man's journey to discover his purpose involves doing exactly what he is afraid of doing.

Therefore, you see many of today's men who are searching for their true purpose take up activities like hang gliding, fire walking, martial arts, and so on. The way most men contact their purpose is by direct confrontation with fear.

If you look at uniquely masculine forms of spirituality, they usually have to do with being right at your edge. Fasting for 40 days and 40 nights; being right at your edge in meditation with some guy whacking you on the back with a stick the moment your attention wanders; being right at the edge with a Zen koan, a paradoxical spiritual question, and no matter how you answer the question your master whacks you. You are being put right at your edge—total terror and frustration.

In more shamanistic cultures a man might ingest psycho-active plants and have terrifying visions, from which he returns whole, victorious and humbled. The masculine form of vision is almost always a confrontation or battle with demons in one form or another.

A man discovers his vision by doing what his heart senses is true, even though he fears it most, and then carrying through with it. If he is terrified of making money, of his success, or of his failure, he must do it. It may mean going out, confronting his fears, going through with what he is afraid to do. His visionary challenge has very little to do with relaxing into who he is, which is the feminine way.

Ultimately, he must relax into who he is. But he must first find his vision. In the Hindu holy book, the Bhagavad Gita, Lord Krishna didn't say to his disciple Arjuna, "Remember me, and relax." He said, "Remember me, and fight." Arjuna was a warrior.

For men, growth usually involves a "holy war" with whatever prevents them from being free. Usually they engage this struggle in isolation or in the company of other men. Once they find their vision, once they are in the process of working it out, they can also embrace life with a woman and share intimate love.

Then they can also relax into who they are, profoundly, because they have disciplined themselves from wandering in distraction. They have used their sword of discrimination to cut away internal bullshit and slay the demons of their inner conflicts so that their heart-purpose is singular. Now they can relax into love without distraction.

So often during the so-called mid-life crisis, men get divorced, leave their family and start something new. If there was a structure in our society where, for several months, a man could release his vocational obligations and household focus, he might not have to leave his family permanently because he could confront his deepest fears and engage his edge in temporary solitude. But in our culture such a vision quest is not supported.

Until men receive their vision and understand their fears, they may always feel self-suppressed and stuck. Life seems like hell to them because they can't do what they really want to do. However, after penetrating through the barriers of their fear, men can incarnate fully. They are no longer fearful. They are finally able to share love without reservation.

Why Does It Seem to Make Things Worse When I Try to Help Him?

If your man is not living his vision, if he is wobbly in his life, then you won't be able to trust him. Since you don't trust him, your own masculine energy comes up to try and save the day.

If he isn't living his vision there is only so much you can do about it. You could help him. You could support him. But basically, it's up to him. And if he is not living it, you can't trust him. You won't trust him. In relation to him, your masculine will come up in order to take care of business and protect yourself. Then, there will be depolarization, defensiveness and lack of trust.

You need to be able to maintain your own wholeness, but part of maintaining your wholeness is participating in the exchange of love in relationship. You can't experience the exchange of love with him unless he is living his vision.

The best way for you to support your man's vision is to let him know how you are feeling. If you see your man not living his vision, if he's just hanging out and not getting it together, you might be tempted to tell him to get off his ass and get it going. But if you do that, you will be bringing him masculine energy and he will resent it.

Instead, try to feel deep down and uncover the primary feeling underlying your anxiety. Maybe you feel like he isn't taking care of you. Perhaps there is a feeling of insecurity, or just an anxiety or inability to relax. Tell him that. Instead of telling him what to *do*, tell him how you *feel*. That way, instead of bringing him masculine energy and making that the issue, you will be bringing him the gift of your feminine sensitivity. This will reflect to him how his irresponsibility affects others.

Whether or not he becomes more responsible is up to him. It is completely out of your hands. If you try to change him, the relationship will only become more depolarized. Gift him with your love, gift him with your happy and radiant feminine energy, and if he doesn't get responsible soon, leave him. There is no reason for you to be a victim of his irresponsibility.

What Can I Expect If My Man Is Just Beginning to Grow Strong?

As your man becomes stronger in his masculine energy, he will become more directed in his life, and you may experience this as a loss of playfulness or sensitivity.

To grow in confidence and strength in the world, a man has to go out there and bust ass. He needs to eliminate distractions from his life, discipline himself with daily goals to meet and not play and engage in conversations which distract from his work.

If you look at men who are very successful at business, art, sports or spiritual practice, you will see that for periods of their lives they have applied themselves totally to the accomplishment of their vision. They have focused their lives and have known what they wanted. They have very firm goals and they eliminate distractions. Men like this are often a pain in the ass in intimate relationships.

For instance, it's great when a man becomes financially or creatively successful, but such men are often very unsuccessful at softness, at feeling, at sensing and responding to your love. If you reject your man's quality of self-centered or project-oriented focus, then he will feel your rejection of his masculine essence.

If you want a man who is very confident and successful but also feeling and sensitive, then find a man who is already strong in his masculine and gift him with the feminine by inviting him into sensitivity. The other way doesn't work. You can't find a sensitive man and then teach him how to be strong in his confidence and success. To do this you would have to animate your masculine energy, which would depolarize the relationship.

Choose a man who is already confident and successful. Or, allow your man to develop his own masculine energy, by himself or in the company of other men.

He is responsible for his own growth, but you can play a part in it. You can find the strength in yourself to support his one-pointedness, including his disregard of those around him, but only for clearly defined periods of time. After this period of total focus he should, of course, be able to embrace you in total love. His presence with you should be full and undivided.

How Can I Teach Him to Receive My Feminine Gifts?

There is a fine line between unhealthy "co-dependence" and serving one another with your gifts. A key to relational healthiness is to give your gifts because you love to give them, not because you are hoping to get something in return. Then, if your man can't receive your gifts, you are still living exactly how you want to live, giving your gifts. Your happiness is not dependent on his ability to receive you. In your happiness, however, you may choose to share your gifts with another man.

What can you do if your man doesn't seem to respond to your feminine gifts? Maybe he just doesn't know how to receive them. In our anti-feminine society, many women don't know how to give their feminine gifts and many men don't know how to receive them. Your man might have some learning to do. Before you decide he is the wrong partner, allow for some learning. Eventually, if he proves incapable of receiving your gift, then you may be inappropriate for each other at this time.

One of the best ways to teach a man how to receive your feminine has nothing to do with any discussion between you. Rather, it involves inviting your man into his body, not verbally inviting him, but inviting him through touch, through sensual communion, through emotions, through sexuality. It involves teaching him the wisdom of the body, the wisdom of the feminine force, the wisdom of subtle, natural energies. The best way to teach him about the feminine is by attracting him into it, not necessarily by talking about it.

This is one unique way that the feminine energy teaches the masculine energy to relinquish its heady one-sidedness and to flow with the energy of love. This is how he learns to receive you.

11

The Ups and Downs of Masculine Sexuality

What Does My Man Feel
When He Stares at Other Women?

When a man sees a woman who fits what he considers attractive, he has an instant bodily response of sexual polarization. It is not an emotional response. It's just like smelling a freshly brewed cup of coffee, seeing a glorious rainbow or smelling the intoxicating fragrance of a flower. It's a moment of thrill, a wave of desire and appreciation.

This kind of attraction has no influence on a man's love for his chosen partner. When your man sees an attractive woman, it does not cause him to remove his love from you. It has nothing to do with love. It is a physical response to the universal force of sexual attraction between masculine and feminine energies.

Why Is My Man So Mechanical During Sex?

As a woman, making love is something that takes place inside of you, close to your heart. Sexual loving involves a feeling of deep emotion. For a woman, the heart, the body, the emotions and sexuality are all intertwined. To participate fully, you must open your heart and body; you must become vulnerable. You are letting somebody inside of you, inviting someone inside of you and opening your essence to that person. It is a very intimate, loving, emotional, sacred and heartfelt event.

By contrast, from a biological perspective, a man's sex organs hang outside his body. They are probably the most superficial sense organ he has, farthest from his heart. For him, sex takes place outside of his body, inside you. He need not open himself nor become particularly vulnerable.

At the physiological level, there is a big difference between men and women relative to sex. For many men, having sex is something like eating chocolate, at least at the physiological level. If you put chocolate against your tongue, it tastes good. It doesn't matter what mood you are in. In fact, sometimes the worse the mood, the better the taste. It doesn't really matter who gives you the chocolate. It's the chocolate you taste. For many men, the pleasure of sex is similar to this.

Sex *could* be as sacred for a man as it is for a woman. But in general, for a woman, it is hard to dissociate sex from emotion. Her feelings about her partner as well as her feelings about herself play a huge part in what sexual intercourse feels like to her.

This isn't true for many men, for whom sex can simply be a very pleasurable bodily activity, like participating in a sport or eating ice cream.

It is not always this way. Men certainly express their deep loving through sex. But at the lowest level of sexuality, men get enjoyment out of genital stimulation and nothing else. In fact, sometimes men just want this kind of sex and are happy to pay a prostitute for it; love has very little to do with it.

Sex to a man could be equivalent to masturbation. It *could* be. It doesn't have to be. But it's sometimes difficult for women to understand where their man is coming from, what he's thinking, what he's feeling. How could he enjoy sex as sport, sex as ice cream, sex divorced from love and emotion?

Likewise, it is difficult for men to understand where a woman is coming from, what she is thinking and feeling. To him, simple sex is a very pleasurable event. He can't understand why she doesn't enjoy emotionless sex, too. He might think, "We're both getting enjoyment." He projects his way of enjoying sex onto his woman and imagines she enjoys sex the same way. It is not necessarily an emotional or spiritual matter. It is simply a pleasurable physical experience. It is joyous even, but physically joyous, like getting a massage, motorcycle driving, sitting in the sun or eating a sweet papaya. They all give bodily pleasure.

Some women experience sex this way, too, but most men experience sex like this. For a man, not to experience sex this way requires effort and learning. Men usually learn sex through masturbation as a teenager. What they learn early on is that sex involves genital stimulation to the point of orgasm. It is often a difficult learning process for a man to experience sexuality beyond this.

The situation is something like if you were trying to do mathematics while sitting on the beach under the warm sun with the cool water lapping up against you while your boyfriend massaged you. It would be hard to get in the mental mood for math while enjoying such bodily pleasure. Likewise, it is hard for a man to get into an emotional mood while enjoying the pleasures of his body.

Men and women are very different sexually. Your gift to a man is to be a *tantrika*, a sacred sexual initiator. Teach him, over time, how to release his mind, come down into his body and feel from his heart while he is in sexual embrace with you. It will be very natural, very inevitable, for you to do that. For him, it may take years of work. Most men operate at the merely physical level of sexuality by default, since our culture supports little sacredness in anything, especially sexuality.

Why Isn't He More Present with Me After He Has an Orgasm?

After most men have an orgasm their sexual desire decreases tremendously, as does their ability to maintain an erection. After orgasm, your man's polarity with you disappears, and he loses the force of connection with you. *For most men, it takes real learning to combine love and sex.* It is a practice that can take months or even years. In order to learn, men must bypass their tendency to have a relatively quick ejaculative orgasm in order to relax into sensitivity and loving.

Orgasm is a profound shift in energy for men. They quickly move from a full energy state to a state of emptiness. It is a sharp decline, after which they fall asleep or lay relatively inactive. The magnetic force of sexual love no longer attracts them into a polarized embrace with you.

For most women, orgasm is not such a drastic shift. A woman might even have several orgasms in a row, with very little depletion of sexual energy or polarization. Most women remain polarized in sexual attraction whether they have an orgasm or not. This is not true for most men.

Therefore, if you want your man to be able to match your sexual capacity, be willing to patiently help him cultivate his ability to bypass or postpone ejaculative orgasms.* Otherwise, expect many nights when you are lying in bed fully polarized in sexual love, while your man lies snoring next to you, depleted and depolarized.

---

* For more information, see David Deida, 1997. *The Way of the Superior Man.* Austin, TX: Plexus.

Why Do Pictures of Naked Ladies Turn Him On So Much?

This is a true story: President Coolidge and his wife, the First Lady, were once inspecting a large government farm. They passed the chicken coop, where the First Lady saw a rooster having sex with a chicken. She looked at the farmer and asked, "How often does that rooster have sex?" The farmer said, "That rooster has sex 20 or 30 times a day." The First Lady sighed and said to the farmer, "Tell that to President Coolidge."

So the farmer walked up to President Coolidge and said, "Mr. President, the First Lady wants me to tell you that this rooster has sex 20 or 30 times a day." President Coolidge thought a moment and asked, "Is it always with the same hen?" The farmer answered, "No. It's with a different hen every time." The president smiled and said to the farmer, "Tell *that* to the First Lady."

In the jargon of biological science, there is a phenomenon called the "Coolidge Effect," named after this famous incident. Sometimes while breeding animals, such as horses or steers, the male will refuse to mate with the same female more than several times. However, if a new female is introduced, he will become refreshed and repolarized, ready for more sex. This is the Coolidge Effect.

Human men love to see strange naked ladies in movies and magazines. At one level, men are just animals, like women are. They respond sexually to novelty, to new women, even in photos and movies. The Coolidge Effect applies to human men just as it applies to roosters, stallions and bulls.

Do All Men Fantasize About Other Women?

Some men never want sex with anyone but their wife. Some women want sex with many different men every day. But after years of counseling both men and women, I would say that, in general, a man's primary sexual fantasy is to have sex with a variety of attractive partners. However, most women are more attracted to depth in a relationship rather than having many sexual partners. A woman's primary fantasy is to share love in a committed relationship with a man of great intelligence, humor and integrity. So, in our culture, the institution of monogamous marriage actually supports most women in their primary sexual fantasy yet deprives most men of theirs.

This is one of the reasons many men resist marriage. They *do* want to get married, in the sense that they want a deep and lasting intimacy, but by doing so they are denying their primary sexual fantasy.

When a man marries, it is understood he is making a sacrifice that a woman is not making. For example, at the wedding, the traditional role of the best man is to make sure that the groom carries through with it. Typically, the groom sweats in anxiousness and the bride is radiant. For a woman, it's often the fulfillment of her heart. For a man, it's often the denial of his inherent desire for multiple partners.

When men are being free with other men, they let their true feelings out. You can see this clearly in gay men. Gay men don't have to compromise their sexual desires because a woman is involved. Before the AIDS crisis, gay men in general had an incredible amount of sex with an incredible number of different partners. In the pre-AIDS days, gay bars and baths were sexual feasts where men could go and have sex with as many partners as they wanted. That's what men love to do. That's what heterosexual men fantasize about doing with women.

Virtually any man who becomes your intimate partner will have a fantasy for sexual variety, even though he is committed to you and your relationship in love. Even if he loves you more than anyone else on Earth, he will probably still have a fantasy involving sex with other women, though he will hopefully choose not to act on it. He *can still* be entirely monogamous in his behavior.

If your man is having an affair, you must take action. Never suppress your feelings and let him do what he wants. Perhaps he is just having sex for pleasure and still totally loves you. But it doesn't matter what he is doing and why he is doing it—you have to be true to yourself.

Find a partner capable of making the kind of agreements you want to live by. You both need to understand each other's needs, each other's bottom line. You must align your relationship toward your highest vision. If your highest vision is love, then the relationship must serve love in every way, providing a context for you and him to grow more and more in your ability to give love, receive love and to be loved.

If he is not capable of truly loving you, if he is not in a full relationship with you, he is certainly not capable of being in a full relationship with someone else, too. Having affairs will not make his relationship with you more full.

The only time you or your man might be able to have more than one intimate relationship is if you had a true and fully loving relationship with each other, and if your relationship with another person did not detract from your ability to be fully committed in love with your partner. But this situation is exceedingly rare.

12

How to Attract Your Perfect Partner

What Makes a Perfect Partner?

Everyone has defects. There is no such thing as a perfect person. No man will ever be able to fulfill you perfectly or love you the way you've always wanted to be loved. There is no fairy tale Prince Charming who will come into your life and sweep you off your feet forever.

If your true purpose is to grow in your ability to love and be loved, then the perfect partner is someone who is also committed to this practice. He may have all kinds of physical or character defects. He will almost certainly have his own obstructions to the vulnerability of complete trust in intimacy. But if he is committed to growing through those obstructions and learning to open his heart more and more with you, then he is the perfect partner.

How Can I Evoke My Man's Passion?

There are various practices men and women can do with one another to awaken their full sexual character. There are ways you can help awaken his masculine energy and ways he can awaken your feminine energy. These practices are based on the principle that the masculine and feminine energies are like magnets. They draw each other out. They each evoke their opposite.

Imagine an incredibly passionate, strong, sensitive, humorous and intelligent man walking up to you, looking deep into your eyes, holding you around your waist and loving you. He sweeps you off your feet. Can you feel it in your body?

If such a man were to embrace you this way, he probably

wouldn't evoke from you a desire to pick *him* up and sweep him off his feet. His masculine energy doesn't evoke your masculine. Rather, his masculine love evokes your feminine swoon. This is the principle of polarity: Each pole has the power to evoke its opposite.

Use this principle to help your man become strong in his sexual character. If you animate your feminine energy, especially in an extreme form, it will evoke his masculine energy, strength and passion.

How Do I Attract a Man Who Cherishes My Feminine Energy?

You always attract a man who accepts yourself as much as you do. If you treat yourself as a woman, and you are rested in your feminine energy, secure in your feminine, pleasured and ecstatic, and in love with your own masculine energy as well, then you will attract a man who honors your feminine, cherishes your feminine and also loves your masculine and feminine.

To the degree you don't accept yourself as you are, if you are needy, you will attract a different kind of man, a man who needs to be needed. If he needs to be needed and then you become whole and no longer need him, he won't want the relationship anymore.

If you don't want to be challenged in the relationship, if you don't want to take on too much self-discipline, you will attract a man who's not too disciplined. In fact, you are going to want a man who's not too disciplined so he doesn't put his discipline on you.

Be honest with yourself and see what you really want in intimate relationship. If you are totally in love with both your internal masculine and feminine and have no resistance to relinquishing your sense of independence in the midst of ecstatic embrace, no resistance to being ravished in love by a man, and no resistance to supporting your man's true direction, then you will attract a man who wants to cherish you as a woman. You will attract a man full of masculine force, whose love for you is full of integrity, passion and humor.

Why Do We Doubt Each Other's Love?

Usually, you attract someone who shares the exact amount of doubt you do. You can be pretty sure that whoever you are in relationship with has the same degree of openness, fear and doubt as you do.

The final confession of fear in your relationship is, "I doubt that you really love me. I don't trust love completely. I'm terrified something is going to go wrong in our relationship." So you could say that to each other, smile, hug and make love. It could be a complete confession of your fears, and you could also transcend it by loving right through it.

A part of you does love him and a part of you is truly terrified of unlove. Intimacy involves facing both of these potentials: total abandonment in love and total abandonment in the fear of not being loved.

When he says, "In a past relationship my partner left me, and now I don't trust that any relationship will work," he is expressing his fear of not being loved. You could meet his honest confession with yours: "I also fear you will leave me, or that it's not going to work out." Then hug him.

Don't get into a dramatic soap opera full of whining and tears. It could be a simple confession. "I have this terror, too. But I can feel your love now." It's not a drama.

This confession of fear is itself a form of intimacy, because you are opening the truth of your hearts to each other. True intimacy involves confessing your fears, but then transcending them in the direct communication of love.

Why Do I Get Bored with Men Who Feel "Safe"?

All of us have blocks to the masculine and feminine energies in ourselves and in our partners. Therefore, we frequently choose a partner who feels "safe."

For instance, imagine a woman who is more comfortable in her masculine energy than in her feminine. She will probably choose a man who carries most of the feminine energy in the relationship so that she doesn't have to. Such a man feels "safe."

For some couples, this kind of relationship works out fine, but only if the woman's true sexual essence is more masculine and the man's true sexual essence is more feminine. This situation is actually quite rare. Most men have a more masculine sexual essence and most women have a more feminine sexual essence.

However, for cultural reasons, especially in the last 30 years or so, women have shifted toward expressing a more masculine persona than their true sexual essence. At the same time, men have expressed a more feminine persona. So today we see a lot of relationships between men who act more feminine than they naturally are and women who act more masculine than they naturally are. Both partners end up feeling dissatisfied with this kind of relationship, even though they feel safe. The man will be too passive for his woman and the woman will be too directive for her man. It isn't emotionally or sexually satisfying to either partner.

When you choose a partner who feels safe, you are probably choosing a partner who has less masculine energy. If your natural sexual essence is feminine, a man with less masculine energy won't be able to fulfill your deep desires in intimacy, though he will feel quite safe to you.

Why Do I Attract Wimpy Men?

If masculine energy is your *predominant* energy, you will attract a man who is less directed and less persistent than you. He may say one thing and do another. This is a man whose masculine is not very strong. Since he has disowned his masculine, he is getting the opportunity to re-own it through his relationship with you.

If you find yourself with a man who lacks masculine integrity, who is wishy-washy and cannot persist in his vision, you can be pretty sure that you predominantly express strong masculine energy. Your highly developed masculine has attracted a man with an underdeveloped masculine who seeks completion through yours.

If you predominantly expressed feminine energy, then you would attract a man who was seeking completion through union with your feminine. His strong masculine would be gifted by your feminine. Rest in your feminine, and you will attract a man rested in his masculine. This is how the natural force of sexual polarity works: The energy you relinquish comes back to you from your partner.

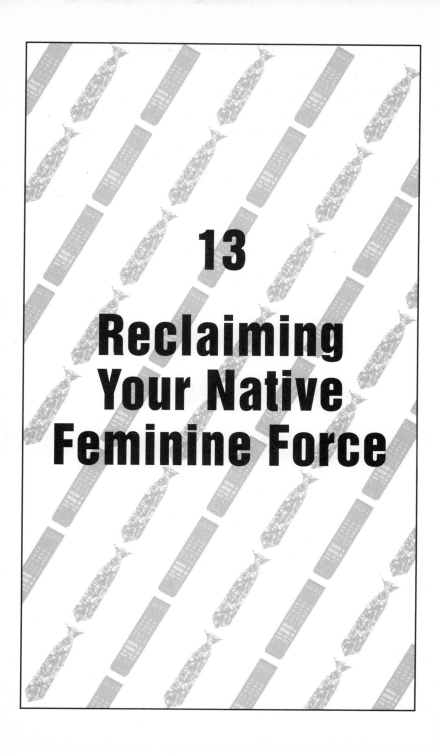

13
Reclaiming Your Native Feminine Force

What Happens When I Reject My Own Feminine or Masculine?

All of us have both masculine and feminine energies. For instance, any time you are eating delicious food and feel, "Mmmmm, this is good," you are in your feminine energy. You are connected to your senses, sensitive to your body's experience.

When you behold a beautiful sunset, when you are in communion with nature, when you appreciate any sensual experience at all, whether you are a man or a woman, in that moment you are in your feminine energy. Some men and women are less comfortable in their feminine energy than in their masculine. Because of the way they were raised, because of their culture, or because of a traumatic experience in their early life, they may disown or reject their feminine energy.

If someone rejects their own feminine, one symptom will be a relative inability to enjoy sensual experiences, including sexuality. Such a person, man or woman, will be hardened to the enjoyment of sensual pleasures. They won't be able to relax and let go. Instead, they will tend to be goal-driven perfectionists, tense, efficient and unable to fully surrender in intimate embrace.

Some people are blocked to their masculine energy. Anyone who has a block to their masculine energy will have difficulty getting anything done. They will flow from one thing to another, being distracted by friends and family. They rarely complete their projects. Or, they may have difficulty breaking an addiction, whether that addiction is to a drug, food or relationship. Very frequently in abusive relationships, for instance, one partner will have difficulty leaving even though it's in her best interest. She has become addicted to the relationship.

If your masculine energy is underdeveloped, you will find it difficult to discipline yourself, to exercise regularly, to set and meet long-term goals and to let go of old relationships.

Why Would a Woman Suppress Her Own Feminine Energy?

The art of polarity does not involve suppression. The woman, for instance, does not need to suppress her natural masculine energy in order to be sexy. The art of polarity involves skillful cultivation of both masculine and feminine energies while consciously relaxing into your heart and body as a man or a woman.

A certain percentage of women naturally prefer to carry the masculine energy in an intimate relationship. In an intimate embrace, for example, some women are more at "home" in their masculine than their feminine energy. However, most women, when relaxed and happy in intimate embrace, naturally move into their feminine energy.

What are women like when they are in their masculine energy? They want to guide the people around them and control their own lives. They don't want help. They prefer to sit down with an agenda and take care of projects rather than open themselves in vulnerable relationships with friends or lovers. Some women are naturally like this. They are most happy and relaxed this way. And all women use this kind of energy at various times throughout the day.

Other women, however, are habitually in their masculine energy but are not happy and relaxed there. They are "stuck." They may be in their masculine energy as a defense mechanism, as a result of internal strife, or from stress put on them by their work. They may also be influenced by social expectations, the way their parents raised them, or a traumatic childhood experience. Something has guided their behavior toward the masculine side of the spectrum. Perhaps they learned to reject the feminine because they experienced pain when they were in their feminine energy as a child: They may have been sexually abused or just mistreated. It is often very difficult for a woman with these kinds of childhood experiences to allow herself to be fully expressed in her feminine energy.

By understanding ourselves we can grow beyond our childhood patterns and the social expectations that limit our ability to enjoy and sustain passion in our intimacies. We can begin to unravel the ways we unconsciously act to deaden or neutralize our relationships. And we can discover ways to magnify the polarity and appreciation between men and women.

What Do I Have to Do to Be Feminine?

Being feminine is not a matter of reaching for something to be, feeling, "Oh my gosh, how do I do that?" It is important to remember that there is nothing outside of yourself to do. It's simply a matter of relaxing and allowing what is already true of you to be fully expressed.

Just relax into your heart, your body and breathe. You will be surprised at how simple it is. It's a matter of relaxing into what is *already* true of you, rather than jumping outside of yourself.

In relationship to men, for instance, the natural feminine force *is* the attractive force. There is nothing that you have to do to make it so. If you walk into a room filled with men, you will feel this charge of polarity. It doesn't matter how many times you have been told you are unattractive. Your natural feminine radiance, your relaxed feminine happiness and your open feminine heart are expressions of universal feminine energy. The attractive force is simply true of you, if you choose to relax into your body as the feminine expression of human life.

Should I Try to Be More Feminine in Order to Attract My Man?

The more one-sidedly masculine your man is, the harder it is to draw him into life with you. If you want a man who is more masculine than you, he will be more directed, more modal, more purposeful, more one-pointed, more concentrated, and more goal-oriented than you. It all comes with the package.

For a man in his masculine, nothing is more attractive than a woman in her feminine. Therefore, just by relaxing into your own feminine your man will naturally be drawn into relationship with you. Don't *try* to attract him. For your own sake, for your own happiness, relax into your own native sexual essence. Relax into your body as you are.

You can do this through your breathing. When you enter your man's masculine head-world, you will notice your breath shifts. You are probably not breathing fully. You are probably breathing high in your chest rather than deep in your belly.

One way to remind yourself to relax as who you are is through your breath. Relax, and continue breathing full and round instead of short and angular. Allow your breath to flow smooth and deep. Breathe in and out of your heart with your belly acting like a bellows, drawing your breath in and then releasing it. This will help center you in your whole body instead of just in your head.

As an experiment, breathe as you imagine a man breathes, with a masculine kind of breath, whatever that means to you. Now, breathe with a feminine breath. Notice the difference. Relax into the breath that feels most at home to your heart. Feel your breath from your heart.

Instantly, your body will soften, your breath will become more round and full and your feminine force will radiate naturally from your heart. This exercise allows your whole body to express the love in your heart. Do it for your own sake, not for the sake of your man—although he will certainly feel your magnified feminine force.

Why Am I Afraid of How Feminine He Makes Me Feel?

The more masculine your man is, the more he will polarize you toward the feminine. If your previous relationships have been with less masculine men, you were polarized only slightly into your feminine.

If you are with a man who is *extremely* masculine, he will polarize you into realms of the feminine with which you may not even be familiar. It may be new territory for you and you might not know how to relax into this new realm; you might not trust your own extreme feminine energy.

There are ways to grow through this. For instance, you could tell him you would like to pretend you are a virgin. You would like him to love you, and be with you, as if you were totally inexperienced. You could feign complete unfamiliarity with what it is to be a woman sexually. He could gently "initiate" you, guiding you slowly, with great care and sensitivity.

If you have never surrendered to your own extreme feminine energy, then, in a sense, you are a virgin at the far outskirts of the feminine. Perhaps you haven't allowed yourself to be ravished in passionate love by a man you trust. You may have no previous experience of this kind of loving. You may have never been polarized by a man to this degree. So make it a special ritual. Play as if you were a kind of "virgin."

Tell your man, "I'd like to trust you to bring me into the deepest parts of my sexuality. But be gentle with me and go slowly, as if I've never experienced this before. I'd like to explore what it means to totally surrender in love as a woman. Take me to the far reaches of sexual ecstasy." Let his masculine polarity bring you to these places.

Such ecstasy involves trusting him with your vulnerability, opening beyond your edges. This ritual is an acknowledgment of trust.

Part of the feminine aspect of sexuality is deep reception. The first step might be relinquishing your need to try to please him. Just go with him, receiving his love and responding spontaneously. Trust him to bring you into ecstasy. An aspect of feminine sexuality involves opening yourself and trusting where he wants to go in loving you passionately. Perhaps he needs to learn to be more sensitive before you can trust him sexually. Take as long as you both need in order to learn how to give and receive deep sexual love.

When he is sensitive, you will find that where he wants to

go is also where you want to go. Later on, you may want to reserve a night for *you* to lead and him to receive and respond. But for now, allow him to polarize you into your unexplored feminine extremes of spontaneously expressed ecstasy and completely abandoned surrender into love.

Why Do I Feel Incompetent When I Relax in My Feminine?

Notice when your inner voice comes up and says, "I am incompetent when I am relaxed in my feminine energy." Your masculine energy may be competent in organizing your schedule and achieving your goals, but your feminine energy is competent in sharing energy, nurturing and radiating the force of life, sensing others, connecting with subtle energy and accessing intuitive knowledge and an immensity of bodily wisdom.

You could begin to re-own this kind of competency, a feeling competency, an intuitive competency, a competency in the flow of unseen energies and elemental forces of nature, and a competency in serving life on Earth with your unique gifts of love.

As you reclaim your power you will encounter resistance to the feminine force in society, in your partner and in yourself. Your man also may devalue the feminine energy, calling it incompetent or irrational. You may encounter dark, shadowy parts of yourself that neither you nor he wants to look at. You will also be evoking parts of himself he may have never fully experienced in relationship.

You may be expressing your feelings and he may say,

"What the hell are you talking about!? You make no sense at all. Just calm down and tell me what you want to do and stop being so emotional about it." You may feel really hurt, but he may not be at home with your style of expression and feeling. He may be more comfortable with your more masculine expression of thoughts and wants.

Your man may become more critical of you as you allow more of your feminine force to express itself. As he learns to trust your spontaneous feminine expression as much as your more organized and controlled masculine expression you will both experience growth in your relationship. But first, learn to trust your own feminine—it is not incompetent, though it expresses itself much differently than your masculine.

Why Is He Afraid of My Emotional Force?

It is difficult enough for a man to embrace his own emotions. Since your emotions are probably much broader and more intense, it is especially difficult for him to embrace yours.

One negative quality of the masculine is its tendency to dissociate from the raw force of life. Avoiding your emotions is one of the ways he dissociates. For most men, it is a crucifixion to enter into life, and that which attracts them into life is the feminine.

Part of your feminine that attracts a man into life is your gift of feeling. But unless a man is very stable in his own practice of love, this gift will pull him off track. Especially in your wilder moods, he is afraid to enter into the chaos of your storm. He may even become disgusted by the more wild aspects of your feminine energy.

Your man is probably not rejecting your emotions, *per se.* Men do not want to be constrained by life—*and your emotions are raw life.* If you are continually expressive of your emotions, you invite your man to embrace one of the most difficult aspects of experience for him to embrace: raw life.

The more you relax in your feminine energy, the more attractive you will be to a man *and* the more you will test his ability to embrace raw life. You become the epitome of everything that is attractive to him in life and everything that repels him from life.

Since men essentially stand outside of life, it confounds them that you are awash in a sea of emotion while they float in a blue sky. It is a challenge for them to leave their blue sky of mind and embrace your rip tide of raw feminine force. A man must become strong in his ability to remain centered and also feel the strong flow of your emotional force.

You are always free to express everything that comes up in you, free to be the wild bitch as well as the radiant goddess. If your man learns to remain centered in his heart, he can learn to remain in relationship with you even in your wildness.

As a woman, you are probably familiar with emotional roller-coaster rides. To most men, these rides may seem like irrational outbreaks of energy or chaotic storms. You may even seem insane to your man. Sometimes your "wild vibe" is so strong you can just walk into the room and your man will suddenly feel, *Uh-oh. Here it comes.* To him, such emotional drama seems unnecessary. He wonders, "Why do you have to do this?"

He is weak if your wild energy makes him leave. He must learn to penetrate your storm with steady love. That's his gift to you. But your responsibility is to stay in your feeling and remain in relationship with him. Don't withdraw. Practice remaining connected with him and with your own core, your own heart, a heart that knows love even in the midst of chaos.

What's the Fastest Way to Cultivate My Feminine Energy?

Relax and breathe. Feel the pleasure of being alive. Learn to give and receive bodily love with your partner, touching each other, gazing into each other's eyes, every day. Make time in your life to participate in raw nature, walking, swimming, roaming the woods or the beach. Listen to music and dance often; spend frequent time in the company of your close women friends; practice giving and receiving love, regardless of your mood, with your intimate friends. Play with children and abandon yourself sexually with your lover, so that your heart expands beyond all limits.

How Do I Develop the Masculine Part of Myself?

The masculine part of your self has the ability to stand outside of your present situation, discriminate which direction is best, and guide the situation in that direction.

To develop your masculine, create a daily schedule and stick to it. Guide your life from your sense of highest good, and discipline your activities, hour after hour, in your chosen direction. Account for every hour of the day. Whatever your mood, stick to your daily disciplines of diet, exercise and work. Cut through all obstructions that arise both internally and in the world around you. Set daily, monthly, yearly and five-year goals. Decide what you have to do today in order to meet your goal. Continually realign your goal with your heart, so that your love is being expressed through your daily activity and so your feminine essence is not lost in this masculine activity.

Shouldn't I Try to Balance My Internal Masculine and Feminine?

In daily life, it is useful to balance your internal masculine and feminine energies. That way you can both direct and nurture yourself. But if you hold on to this internal "equality" between your masculine and feminine energies even within the play of your intimate relationship, then you prevent ecstatic reunion from occurring in its full, sexually polarized form.

If a couple desires to experience spiritual ecstasy, then they should allow their reciprocal sexual characters to freely manifest in their partners. As a woman, allow your man to carry the masculine energy during moments of polarized sexual intimacy. Then, you can experience the blissful reunion of your feminine with his masculine. Learn to trust him as well as your own feminine energy.

Deep trust of your feminine means resting in pure radiance: mindless, edgeless, heart-energy, shining beyond words with no limited direction. Allow yourself to surrender into this love-energy. A woman who surrenders into this energy is ecstatic. Your radiant love is obvious—and that's what the masculine is moved to embrace.

Be careful what kind of practices you do. If you practice equalizing your internal masculine and feminine energy so that you are no longer clearly defined as a feminine sexual character, then you won't attract a polarized masculine partner. If the energy you put out is equally masculine and feminine, a man will not feel you as a *woman*. He might feel your balance as a person, but he won't be moved to embrace you as his chosen source of feminine love.

Since Men Don't Seem to Have Much Integrity, Why Should I Trust Them?

If you mistrust men you will animate your own masculine energy instead of trusting that a man will be there for you. And if you animate your own masculine energy, then your potential partner will feel you more as a friend than as a polarized lover. Therefore, one of the first steps in attracting or cultivating a man's true masculine energy of integrity is to trust it.

You may have been hurt by someone's masculine energy in the past, but you must still learn to trust. There are good men and less good men, but masculine energy, in itself, is one form of divine or universal energy. As a woman, you will attract a man who freely gifts you with his masculine energy—with his passion, his success, his discrimination and his love—when you learn to trust masculine energy. By simply trusting the masculine force you will either attract an appropriate man or evoke authentic masculine energy in your present partner.

Trusting that the universe will deliver authentic masculine

energy to you means relaxing in your feminine. If you doubt that a man exists whom you could totally trust, it will prevent you from relaxing fully in your feminine. The men you attract will not be fully relaxed in their masculine. They will be divided inside, as you are. Your mistrust will actually prevent a trustable man, full of integrity, from appearing in your life.

If you don't trust men, then you won't fully let go in intimacy. If you won't fully let go, you will experience pain. The clench around your heart hurts. Being afraid to let go is painful.

Anytime you notice yourself talking negatively about men, or doubting that a good man exists, be aware of your feeling of doubt. This feeling will keep you holding on to your own masculine energy. Because you doubt that the universe will provide you with a good man, you may not quite allow yourself to free-fall into your native feminine energy.

Trust letting go more and more. Find out what happens when you let go into your feminine energy of radiant and doubt-free love. You may find that as you let go of your doubt and fall into your native feminine energy, a man will appear who reciprocates you or your present partner will suddenly begin to gift you with his native masculine energy. His gift of integrity and your relaxation into your own feminine force go hand in hand.

14

Deciding If
He Is the
Right Man

Is It Possible for Partners to Grow in Different Directions?

The one masculine trait that transcends a man's purpose is his connection to truth. If your man's connection to truth remains strong, his purpose might change as he aligns himself more and more with truth. For instance, for five years he may be totally dedicated to a business, then give it up and move into a monastery. Although this might look like a completely different purpose, this may be the closest way—for the present time—for him to live his truth.

If you ever wonder about your man's new direction in life, ask yourself: Do you feel in your heart that his new direction is more aligned with truth or farther from truth?

Even if his new direction is aligned with *his* truth, is it aligned with *your* truth? You might not want to change in the same way that he is changing. How do you bridge that gap? Honestly, come into touch with what your truth is, what your heart truly wants.

Temporarily separate yourself from him to discover your own desire. Naturally, as a woman who loves her man, you will be moved to embrace him. However, you may have a conflict between where he is going and where you want to go.

While you are apart from him, feel in your heart in whatever way works for you. It may be through talking with other women, through ritual, silence or spending time in nature. Discover what is the fullest expression of your heart. What would satisfy your heart the most?

If his truth has carried him in a direction compatible with what would satisfy and fulfill your heart, then your relationship remains viable.

It sometimes happens that two people continue growing

and their relationship changes. This is not necessarily negative. In their growth, one person's truth may lead their daily life in one direction and another person's in another direction. Sometimes these different directions are temporary and sometimes they last a lifetime.

How Can I Leave Him When I Still Love Him?

What you feel and what you should do aren't necessarily the same; it is possible to love a man totally yet walk away from him. If the relationship is not appropriate, you can remain in love and still bring a relationship to an end. Your love, your heart and your connection to God can be full and true, even while you are acting in this difficult circumstance.

Your head is your center of thinking; your heart is your center of emotional feeling; and your belly is your center of action. Your belly, just below your navel, is the place from which your action springs, your center of gravity. In Japanese culture it is called the *Hara* and in Chinese the *T'an-Tien*. By relaxing into your navel area you learn to center yourself in dance and martial arts. This navel area is your center of power—the power to do.

Your heart may be flowing with feeling for a man, but your navel doesn't have to follow that flow. You are free to act decisively and choose to leave a man even though you have strong feelings for him. You don't have to shut down your feelings in order to turn your navel and move in another direction. It's okay to love a man yet decide not to be in intimate relationship with him. It's okay to turn from a man that you love and open yourself in love with someone else who will be a better partner for you.

Women are usually more moved by their feeling center than their action center, so it is difficult for them to walk away from a man they love. Most men are the opposite. They listen to their feelings very little. They are usually more involved with doing and thinking than with emotion. It is usually easier for men to walk away from a relationship.

As a woman, your balance is to remain in your feeling but act in accordance with your highest good, your deepest wisdom. Listen to your close circle of trusted friends. They usually can reflect what is best for you. Feel deep in your heart. Ask your highest self for guidance. Even though you love a man, it may be best to actively turn away from him, even as you continue to feel love for him.

Why Can't I Let Go of My Old Relationship?

Your heart has a memory for love. It stays in love with someone until that love is replaced by new love. Even if you have broken up with your past partner, if you really loved him, if there was a deep sharing of love even though it was also painful, then there will be a part of your heart that remains in love with him.

Your heart loves. It doesn't make decisions. Your heart is open or not. If it's open and in love with him it will remain so until you discover a new love of at least the same depth and intensity.

Don't feel guilty about being in love with your old boyfriend, even though you know it's best not to be with him. You will need to experience love as intensely as you did with him in order to let him go. That could be love of a new man, love of yourself or love of God.

People sometimes spend 30 years loving someone who has died, or loving someone who they broke up with and haven't seen since. That's because they haven't allowed themselves to open up enough to feel love to that depth again.

Will I Ever Stop Fearing That I Will Lose Him?

To a certain extent, all of us have doubt, all of us fear potential loss. We fear it not only in relationships, but in our lives. There is always a little tension. No matter what we have, or how good life is, we never completely relax. Part of us knows that whatever we have we can also lose.

There are, of course, moments when we completely relax. But very often, we may have a nagging sense of insecurity about our relationship. We don't trust it. We're not certain.

Nothing is permanent. Everyone you know is going to die. That person you love so intimately is going to die, eventually. This feeling of loss, of feeling unfulfilled, is felt within every relationship. There is nothing wrong with this feeling.

Our practice of intimacy involves learning to love through our fear of loss. Our fear doesn't mean we are in a bad relationship; all relationships end. It means embracing your man with the full knowledge that it isn't going to last. Your relationship is temporary. He will die, you will die, or the relationship could come to an end for many reasons, even later today or tomorrow.

You will lose everyone you love. The practice of true intimacy involves opening your heart even while you are aware of the temporary nature of relationship.

How Can I Choose the Right Man?

First choose a man with purpose. Second, determine whether you trust his specific purpose. If you are with a man who has purpose, and if you trust his purpose, then you will feel free and relax into your own natural sexual essence. You can also freely offer him support for his purpose.

But if you don't trust his purpose, you won't want to support it. Then he will grow to resent you and feel you are at odds with him. Very little turns a man off more than when his woman negates his purpose. Your negation need not necessarily be verbal. You can nonverbally send your man a message that you don't agree with his direction in life, and he will pull away from you. If you don't trust your man's direction, the relationship will inevitably fail.

Remember the following questions when choosing whether or not to be with a man. First, does he know what he wants in life? He must have a purpose, or he will not be able to offer you his full force of love. Second, do you trust his purpose? Choose a man whose purpose in life will serve you. Choose a man with whom you can relax because you trust his integrity, direction and strength. Choose a man whose heart's desire is aligned with yours.

How Long Should I Wait for Him to Change?

This is a key to deciding whether a man is right for you: As he is right now, can you fully trust him? Or do you think that you could change him into a man you could trust? As soon as you find yourself thinking that you could change him, you are in trouble.

If a man is not *already* living a life that you would wed to yours, then do not commit in relationship, hoping he will change. It is fine to desire change and growth in a relationship, but you must trust him, as he is right now, in order to provide a *foundation* for growth in relationship and a basis for the practice of love. If you do not trust him as he is now, you don't really *have* an intimate relationship.

So choose a man you can trust. Serve him in his growth so you can continue trusting him. But if you really don't trust him as he is, then he will feel it. If you are waiting for him to change before you can trust him, you are locking yourself into a no-win situation.

Trust is the starting point of the practice of intimacy, not something to hope for in the future. In any case, if you find yourself staying in a relationship because you think your man might change, you are making a mistake.

Is It Easier for Men or Women to Leave a Relationship?

The masculine energy always contemplates going deeper into a relationship or leaving it. The feminine, however, is always opening to love or closing. If a woman doesn't have strong enough masculine energy, then all she can do is open or close. If she is in a relationship that causes her a lot of suffering and doesn't have sufficient masculine energy to tell her when it is time to leave, then she can only open or close. When the loving is really good her heart opens; when it is bad her heart closes. But she never really gets up and leaves for good. Many women in problematic relationships close down emotionally, but find it difficult to leave, once and for all.

Women in particular, and men with more feminine energy, will often stay in painful relationships longer than is healthy. Women without sufficient masculine energy might stay in an inappropriate relationship for years and years, opening and closing, opening and closing. Her friends may tell her the relationship is doomed. They may tell her the man is abusing her and that she should leave. But she can't. She hopes that he will change, and she remains in place, suffering and then feeling loved, over and over.

Even when physically abused, it is hard for many women to leave a relationship. Such a woman says, "He really loves me, and I really love him. I know he's trying to change."

Someone may say to her, "But your nose is broken and your eyes are black and blue." Yet she responds, "It really hurts. I don't know what to do. I do love him. I don't know what to do. He needs me. I know he loves me. He'll change." To other people it's obvious what to do. "Go. Get out."

Love is most important to the feminine. In general, as long as a woman feels love for a man and from a man, the other aspects of the relationship won't be enough to cause her to leave. That would mean letting go of the love she feels. It requires a strongly developed masculine energy to end a relationship in which love still flows.

The feminine will virtually never let go of love. Many women who have tried—and failed—to end a relationship in which they felt love for and from their partner, even though they may have been abused by him can attest to this. It's really difficult to leave a relationship with a man you love, even though it's painful.

The feminine in a woman will not let go of the love she presently feels. The masculine in a woman will all too readily let go. Masculine and feminine are balanced by the other. Neither is complete in and of itself.

The masculine often contemplates leaving a relationship at the first sign of difficulty. The feminine often stays in a relationship far longer than is appropriate.

What Is the Bottom Line in a Relationship?

Each of us must decide how much unnecessary suffering we will endure. Too often a relationship goes on for years, staying in the same place of pain, only to finally break up.

To help us determine when to leave a relationship, it is often very helpful for intimate partners to make a "Bottom Line List." At the top of the list you write, "I love you." Then you list your "bottom lines."

For instance: "I will not stay with you unless you are able to support yourself financially. I will be with you if and only if you are learning to support yourself without asking anybody for money. I will see you are learning this because within three weeks you will cease asking anybody for money."

Or, "I will not stay with you unless you are able to listen to me for several minutes without turning away."

Your partner makes the same kind of list. You each list your requirements for remaining in partnership, and you also use time limits, remembering that people need time to change. After you exchange lists you may need to negotiate certain points.

Now you have a contract. It's just like a marriage contract or a premarriage contract. Remember that the requirements you list are requirements that serve love in the relationship. Your requirements should not only serve you, but they should serve your partner as well.

For instance, it doesn't serve either of you when you support his lack of competency. So feel in your heart, what would serve him? Be concrete. Write this down as a bottom line.

Make your agreements, put time limits on them and stick to them. If your present partner cannot live up to your agreement, find someone who does. You could have any partner you want—you have the partner that you have now because you are holding on to him in some way.

Anytime you notice yourself hoping that your man will change, you are in the "battered woman's syndrome" now. Anytime you think, "He will change," but the way he is now isn't good enough for you, then you are presently in an abusive relationship. The warning bells should go off any time he is abusing you today while you hope that he will change tomorrow. It is okay to want your partner to change, but only if the way he is today is good enough for today. You are both growing.

Suffering is part of any intimate relationship, but staying with an abusive man, or a weak and undirected man, is not. You may choose daily to be with a man like this, but it is not a necessary choice.

Should I Leave My Man If He Is Addicted to Drugs?

You cannot trust a man who is actively addicted. You might *love* a man who is addicted, but you can't fully trust him. If he doesn't have power over his own direction, how could you trust him with yours? If he doesn't have the strength to guide his own life, how could you trust him with yours? He hasn't surrendered his life to a Higher Power and hasn't taken control of himself.

You might love such a man. You might feel very drawn to him and want to be with him. You might feel loved by him. But you cannot trust him, and you cannot trust your life with him.

If his addiction doesn't impinge on his happiness, freedom and loving, then it is your problem, not his. But if it inhibits him in his happiness or in his ability to give love, then he needs to wake up.

You can't condemn him for being in a unique moment of learning. His life may be unfolding perfectly for him, but you don't have to trust him as a suitable partner, as someone with whom you share your life. And if you don't trust him, you can expect that he will feel it. He will be hurt and will pull back.

To make such a relationship viable, clearly define the aspects of behavior he needs to change for you to be able to trust him. You can oblige him, through your love, to straighten out his life, because you cannot trust him as he is: addicted.

You need to answer this question for yourself: Is he the kind of man now—today, not tomorrow—with whom you are willing to commit your life and growth?

Should I Stay or Should I Go?

By fully developing our masculine and feminine energies, we can remain open in committed love with our present partner and also be willing to risk everything for the sake of growth. We can be willing to lose the security of our relationship and instead trust in the process of love. We can live our reality, what we really want to do, and face the consequences with an open heart. We can relax and love without becoming dependent on our partner. We can decide if our present relationship is actually serving us, and we can act accordingly. We do not stay in a relationship longer than our real growth indicates, nor do we leave merely because the going gets rough.

15

Succeeding in the Real Practice of Intimacy

How Can I Change Myself?

It is important to understand what you can change and what you cannot change about yourself. If you are Caucasian, you can squint your eyes and look a bit Asian, but it won't make you Asian. If you wished you were black instead of white you could go out in the sun and get a little darker, but it won't make you black. There is some flexibility, but not enough to change you into something you are not.

The personality is also relatively fixed. It can change a little, but basically it is what it is. Some people believe our personality is shaped by the astrological position of the planets at the time of our birth. Some people think past karma and past lives, gave shape to our present personality. Others believe our early childhood experiences shape our personality.

There are many ways of looking at it, but the bottom line is that your personality is more or less fixed. True growth does not involve changing your personality. It involves learning to love, no matter what your personality is.

You could be grossly deformed physically. You could be born without arms and legs. No amount of positive thinking will give you arms and legs. But you could still learn to love and be free and happy even though you had no arms and legs.

Our mission is to learn to love completely even though we have certain physical and personality characteristics. You might be an angry, challenging, insecure person for the rest of your life. It could become very humorous to you, a source of great amusement in your relationships, and not interfere at all in your love and work with people.

Your personality characteristics are what they are. They may change slightly and they may not. Whether they change or not isn't as important as learning to love. You do not have to change yourself, but you can learn to be present and open and loving just as you are.

Will I Ever Find a Man Who Gives Me the Love That I Want?

One of our basic emotional assumptions in intimacy is the feeling, *You don't love me.* All of us have a "button" that is occasionally pressed by our partner which makes us feel, *That person doesn't love me.* The "I'm not being loved" button is one of the most destructive buttons in intimate relationships because it is frequently pressed completely by accident. Our feeling of not being loved has nothing to do with our partner. We are feeling our own closure to love.

For instance, many men can suddenly switch from an intimacy mode to some other mode. Your man is with you in intimacy one moment. Suddenly, the phone rings, a football game comes on TV, or a thought comes to him—and he's gone.

You may feel hurt or rejected because he turned away and forgot you. Your expression of hurt may make him feel constrained, unable to do what he wants. He may even feel resentful and angry toward you.

Much physical abuse of women by men, and also emotional abuse in the form of anger for no apparent reason, is based on this: Men tend to feel constrained by life and especially by their woman.

As a woman, the root meter or radar in your heart is, "Am I being loved or am I not being loved?" As a woman, you are very sensitive to the shift from being loved to not being loved. You are very aware of when your man switches from one mode to another.

Men also have a meter, but it doesn't work the same way. The meter in most men measures, "Am I free or am I constrained?" That's why men get unbelievably angry at things that seem ridiculous to women. For instance, many men will go crazy when they are trying to fix something. If it doesn't go perfectly well, they will start yelling and swearing, "Goddamnit!"

When your man's attempt to fix something becomes frustrating, he immediately feels very constrained. He feels constrained by a screw, or whatever won't work or fit. Because his root meter is sensitive to constraint, the screw gets stuck and his meter flashes: constraint, constraint, constraint. He goes bonkers.

When men and women are in an intimate relationship, there is a feedback cycle between their two "meters." He begins to feel more constrained by your emotional needs in the relationship, by your sensitivity to lovingness. And this sensitivity to lovingness is more and more jarred by his resentment and dissociation from you, his response to feeling constrained.

These buttons get pressed frequently in relationships. All he has to do is feel a little constrained and he will pull away. He pulls away, your meter goes off and you feel unloved. You pull away and he feels a "problem" that needs to be fixed, so he feels even more constrained. The cycle goes on and on.

A large transformation takes place in your intimacy when you realize that your partner has no control over his reactions. When you realize that both of you react automatically to emotional "buttons" that became part of you as children, then you are relieved of much guilt or blame.

If you take away a toy from a very young child because he is hurting himself with it, the child may start demanding,

"Give me my toy! Give me my toy!" He might kick you in the shin and run away. Naturally, you wish the child wouldn't do this. You might talk to him, or give him a consequence for his behavior, or hold him and give him loving attention. However, you don't assume the child purposely acted this way to hurt you and turn away from him. He is only a child. He is learning to love, share and communicate. You feel moved to help the child learn.

It helps to look at your partner this way. You can see he is only being reactive. One of his buttons, one of his childhood wounds, has been pressed. He reacts like he did as a child, communicating in words and actions, "You don't love me! If you did, you would do what I want!"

Suppose your man turns away from you to play with one of his "toys." Instead of collapsing in your own feeling of, *You don't love me*, you could notice, *There it is. He's getting distanced into a mode again.* You can relax in your heart and serve his growth rather than assume he doesn't love you. Just because he kicks you in your emotional shin doesn't mean you should kick him back or run away.

Each of us has a child within that responds the way we did as a child. "Give me my toy! Give me your love! If you don't give me more attention I won't give you my love!"

This inner child responds when our buttons, our childhood wounds, get pushed. Our feminine button gets pushed when we feel unloved; our masculine button gets pushed when we feel constrained and not free to do what we want. In response to feeling unloved or constrained, we act like little children. "If you don't give me the love (or freedom) that I want, then I'm going to collapse or close down or leave you."

No man is capable of *always* giving you the love that you want. When your inner child doesn't get its way it will want to run away, collapse or kick back. Intimacy, like parenthood, is a practice that requires giving love to your partner even while he is pushing your buttons or kicking your shins. Love begets love. Punishment and withdrawal without love do not provide the basis for trust and real growth in intimacy.

How Can I Get the Love I Used to Have?

At the beginning of a new intimate relationship love is very graceful. You don't have to do a lot to maintain it. Both of you give and receive. It's a beautiful dance. We think love should always be like that. But actually, love is an action. You learn to love. It takes practice.

How do you practice relocating love when it feels like love has been "lost?" First, become familiar with your inner doubts and fears, the whole dynamic that cuts off love. Then, you learn to locate love in your heart even under difficult circumstances. It helps to set aside time every day to practice reconnecting with your love. During this time you may pray, dance or meditate. Do whatever it takes to contact the love in your heart. With practice, you can grow in your ability to love.

Love is not something you have or don't have. Love is something you do. It is not something that comes to you. It is something you are giving or refusing to give, moment by moment.

Most people have felt moments of grace when their heart opened and love poured. It may have been spiritual love, God love. It could have been love for a child, a friend or a lover. Your heart might have even opened while looking at a great work of art.

These moments illustrate your innate capacity to love. You need only open your heart and you *are* the force of love. The practice of intimacy is to stay open even during difficult moments. It isn't about getting love and holding on to it.

Love is who you are and what you do when you are not closing your heart. The practice of intimacy is to stay open as love.

How Do I Grow in My Ability to Love?

In any moment, you are either separating yourself from others and from the world, or opening and connecting in relationship. Be aware of the tendency to create distance between you and others. To practice love, simply stay in direct relationship and notice your tendency to pull away and withdraw from love and life.

Do you pull back when your man says certain things? Do you close down when he acts in certain ways? Do you withdraw from him when he withdraws from you? Intimate relationship is a very specific form in which to practice love, but all relationships test our love and give us an opportunity to gift with love.

The more you mature in the practice of love, the more giving you will be in relationships with your intimate partner as well as your friends. Even when they hurt you, you do not pull away or close down. As you practice love, you grow in your ability to stay open, present and connected in relationship, even when you feel hurt or angry. This open connectedness *is* love.

What Should I Do When
My Relationship Feels Hellish?

When you first fall in love your heart opens and you love everyone you see. Do you know that feeling? During difficult times, you can practice opening your heart like this. It is not always easy to do. But in order to live through the more hellish parts of a relationship, you will need to exercise your capacity to love. You can practice *doing* love, even though other emotions may arise in you at the same time.

You don't have to be namby-pamby, always saying, "I love you." You might be arguing or crying, but it's good to have a little thread attached to your loving self so you can always remember why you are with your man to begin with.

Your ongoing practice is to continue loving as you take each step along the path of intimacy. And the first thing you will confront on this path is the boulder of doubt—"Does he really love me?"

Don't avoid doubt. Love *through* it. Don't allow yourself to be overwhelmed by doubt, rather, let doubt come up *and love*. "I'm totally afraid, and I love you so much, I want to work through this." Continue to relocate your love, and it will shine through your doubt, so that eventually your doubt becomes obsolete, useless.

The feeling of love is always in your heart, but you have to literally relocate it. Your mind will go into other areas: "What will he do in the future? Will he take me into account?" Just relocate your love. You don't have to stop doing other things. Just relocate love. It's always in your heart.

Where was your love before your man came into your life? Was it floating 50 feet away from you? Has this man come along and pushed love into you? No. Love was always in you. He's just your excuse for loving.

We use our partner as an excuse to love. But we need to become responsible for always locating our love, whether our partner is loving or not.

It's a practical exercise. In your day-to-day life make time to relax, relocate and connect with the loving in your heart. Meditate on love; feel into love; magnify love by relaxing into it. Imagine you are in your lover's arms. Your body is opening. Your heart is radiating love. You are making love, embracing love, breathing love. Set aside time and meditate like this, basking in the force of love. Practice relaxing your body in the energy of love, especially when your relationship feels hellish.

How Do I Get Rid of the Tension in My Relationship?

There is always a conflict between men and women in intimate relationships, a subtle tension that simultaneously attracts and repels. It may feel like a conflict, perhaps, but it is strangely pleasurable, too. It is a constant interplay of opposing forces which rarely comes to rest. The only time it comes to rest is when there is no sense of an other, such as in meditative states, in deep sleep, and in the ecstasy of sexual love-union when there is no feeling of separation. In these states, there is no polarized conflict. But as long as there is any sense of separation or difference between you and your lover, there will be a subtle tension between the forces of masculine and feminine.

Furthermore, the extreme intimacy we seek is also the intimacy we fear. We fear losing our sense of independent self in relationship, but we also desire to lose ourselves in the ecstasy of deep love. Complete union with the one we love is therefore what we most desire and most fear.

We cannot entirely rid our intimate relationship of tension. To practice intimacy, we must learn to embrace the constant, subtle tension between masculine and feminine forces. We must also relax through the paradoxical tension of our heart and understand that the complete union in love that we most seek involves the loss of self we most fear.

Should I Tell Him How Afraid I Am?

Nothing makes you more intimate than allowing your resistance, fear and anger to come up in the midst of love. This *is* intimacy. It doesn't block intimacy. It creates intimacy. Holding in your feelings blocks intimacy. Instead, express your true feelings and trust the process of love.

For instance, you might say to your man, "I feel myself opening to you but I'm afraid of becoming needy. I don't want to lose my own center." In this moment, you are being intimate, dealing with your feelings, talking about them and feeling them together with your man, yet also truly expressing your fear.

Intimacy has its own intelligence. Love its own power. They will transform your old patterns. But you have to be willing to sacrifice your self-containment to allow love to do its work. You have to be willing to let go of control.

You open yourself to receiving love by giving love. You

invite trust from your man by trusting him. If you're holding back he'll hold back. You will become involved in a battle of holding back.

Trust love. Trust that in your love with a man you could bring up how insecure you feel. See how far giving your trust to a man will go. See how far giving your trust to love itself will go. But be intelligent about it. If it's going to a negative place then stop it. But if it's going to a positive place, let your doubts and fears come up and continue to trust love.

If you feel something strange is going on between you, instantly bring it up. Don't blame him. Just say, "I'm feeling uncomfortable," and let love do its work. Let your body relax into love. Let your breath become a breath of love, a trusting breath, a full and soft breath. Stay connected to love and hold nothing back.

Will He Always Bring Out the Worst in Me?

The practice of intimacy requires you to face your deepest inner demons and fears. When you are in love with a man, every single part of you that has yet to be totally infiltrated by love will rise to the surface like oil on water.

To be capable of love means allowing all your stuff—and all his stuff—to come up. Your fear will come up. So will your feeling of being needy and dependent. So will your anger. Consciously allow this to be part of the relationship.

You know those electric bug zappers? That's what love is like. If you are in love with somebody, you can allow your inner garbage to be attracted to the surface, be zapped and then vaporized by love.

Sometimes it takes a little longer than a millisecond to zap it, but it does happen. However long it takes, the process of love will dissolve old emotional stuff. It's not exactly comfortable, but you could acknowledge that it's part of the package of love. No matter how "bad" your stuff is, you can continue to practice loving. The force of love itself will, over time, serve to dissolve the "worst" of you.

How Can I Avoid the Negative Feelings That Come Up in Intimacy?

Many people try to concentrate on just feeling the positive aspects of being in a relationship and avoid the negative feelings. But you can't avoid either of them in a relationship. Part of being intimate is seeing and feeling your emotional stuff come up, as well as his. Seeing and feeling your hidden emotional needs contributes to your growth. You can only avoid negative intensity by avoiding intimacy, or by avoiding relationship altogether.

Those parts of ourselves we are not ready to accept are the parts that will cause us to withdraw from relationship when they start coming up. Intimate relationship brings everything up, some parts of which we are not yet ready to face. It's good to find out what those parts are. Then we know that when the relationship brings those parts up we will feel like turning away from the relationship.

Nobody *wants* to feel the negative feelings that arise in the midst of deep intimacy. Nobody wants to see their own psychological garbage that limits their gift of love. But intimacy itself is a call to growing through these parts of yourself.

At some point, when you are ready, allow yourself to feel the intense negative emotions that inevitably arise in a relationship. It's important to be in a relationship with somebody who you actually trust will grow with you. Then when these feelings come up, breathe through them, relax through them in direct relationship with your partner. Continue to love through them as they come up.

Will I Always Fail in My Relationships?

Some people have all kinds of relationships throughout their lives, none really fulfilling, and then they die. You may have spent half your life without a fulfilling relationship. Maybe now you have grown to a place of being able to attract and contribute to a fulfilling relationship. It has been quite an education for you.

In the past you were not yet full. But now you are capable. Remember that you will *always attract someone as capable of loving as you are.* You only sabotage yourself if you close down because you don't want to be hurt again. If you do close down you will attract a man equally afraid of intimacy.

To begin a successful intimacy, be willing to experience past hurt and remain open to new love. Acknowledge your history of pain, but remain available to love. Then, the man you attract will also be willing to love, regardless of his past pain.

Is It Possible to Achieve a Perfect Relationship?

A perfect relationship is not a relationship that is perfectly fulfilling. It is a relationship that is growing. There will be times in any relationship when you can't stand each other, but this doesn't mean it's a bad relationship.

The more you trust and the more you love the bigger the demons that will come up. For example, the more you relax into your feminine, the more you will become like Kali, the goddess of destruction. When you get angry, you may really go wild.

A full relationship is not always peachy; there may be disagreements and fights on a regular basis. But if it's a full relationship, then everything happens in the context of your commitment to love. You let it all out and find out if you are capable of growing beyond it. Sometimes you don't know if you are going to make it through, but you persist. You persist in observing your own stuff and in practicing love.

Intimate relationship is an action. It changes over time. It's not as if you *have* a relationship. Rather, your relationship is an ongoing, daily practice.

For example, if you do hatha yoga, you might pull a muscle and for days do yoga with a stiff leg. In the "yoga" of your relationship, you may have an interaction that wounds you for days. It doesn't mean you have a bad relationship; the yoga could still be good. It will just be painful. The yoga, the practice, is to continue discovering love, relaxing into it and giving it, no matter how painful the circumstances.

Sometimes the pain is so intense that you feel totally consumed by suffering. With persistent practice, you can grow in your ability to remember love even during those times.

What drew you to your partner in the first place? Love.

Love itself. Reorient to love itself. Re-remember love itself. Then, practice gifting from this feeling of love. It is a real practice to learn to remember this when you are seething in anger or when you are hurt and feel rejected. A "perfect" relationship is a relationship that supports you and serves you and your partner in this practice of love.

Why Is Loving So Painful?

All of us would like love to be easy, but it is often difficult to love, especially when others are not loving you. It is difficult to love when your relationship reveals your hidden fears and unmet needs.

It is not possible to be in an intimate relationship without experiencing moments of suffering and pain. Some people falsely equate growth with eliminating suffering. Some people believe that the more you grow the less pain you will feel in relationship.

There is a certain amount of pain that can be avoided when you become conscious of the principles of love, polarity and good communication. But love allows all of our hidden aspects to rise to the surface and be purified. This purification process is often painful. In this sense, the greater the love the more effective the purification. Therefore, even though the love may be great, so may be the pain. Perhaps the people who have learned to love the most have also felt the deepest wounds. You may have a belief that the more you grow the less you will suffer the wounds of love; but this is not necessarily true.

You may believe: "If I enter into a new relationship and

feel as much pain as I have in past relationships, then I must not be growing. I must have not learned anything." This belief may prevent you from living in intimacy.

You and all those you love are in the process between birth and death. Your lover is going to die. The knowledge of death in the midst of love is a kind of crucifixion. What's the use? You fall in love with people who are all in the process of dying. How much more crucifixion do you want? To think that there is an alternative is a delusion. Everyone you love will die someday.

In true intimacy there is always suffering. But the heart can be open to giving and receiving love even while suffering, even in the midst of crucifixion. It is this knowledge of love, this certainty that you are love, that love is not compromised by death, that is truth. There is suffering, but there is also truth, which is love. The great spiritual figures in human history have often suffered tremendous crucifixion in the midst of their loving.

Those you love are going to disappear. To deny this is to deny the essence of humanity. It is a crucifixion to allow yourself to get in a relationship with someone who will certainly leave you, sooner or later. There is pain in the knowledge that he is not going to be with you forever and that he is not going to love you all the time. He might not even love you most of the time—he probably doesn't love himself most of the time, so certainly he won't be able to love you most of the time.

As a lover, you are choosing to embrace someone who is going to die as well as someone who isn't always going to be able to love you. You are choosing someone who, because he has unresolved childhood patterns, will be re-living his drama with his parents in the relationship with you. If he was insecure about the love he got from his mother and father, he will be insecure about your love. He will continue to want from you what he wanted most in his childhood and never got. You, too, will want from him that what you never got from your parents.

Loving someone who is dying, someone who is not always going to love you back, committing in intimacy with someone who will repeatedly and unconsciously hurt you due to his childhood patterns—if this isn't a type of crucifixion, what is? But this crucifixion is only the platform for forgiveness. In the midst of death and suffering, can we return to the knowledge of love?

Why Should I Commit to Intimacy If It Is So Painful?

The masculine in each of us is fond of perfection and freedom from constraint. This is why men, in general, don't like the idea of marriage and resist intimate commitment. Men sometimes refer to their wife or marriage as a "ball and chain." You, as a woman, might also ask yourself, "Why would I want to be constrained in an intimate relationship again?" You might wonder this especially if your past relationships have been painful.

Eventually, a realization may dawn. Yes, a relationship is limited and painful—but it's the perfect place to practice incarnating love. It eventually becomes clear to you that love is what you are here to do, and that an intimate relationship provides you with a vehicle for growth in love. When you realize this, you can make a full commitment in love, knowing its inevitable limitation and pain—just as knowing that birth is a commitment to inevitable death.

Every experience comes in the form of a pair. You can't experience physical pleasure without also experiencing physical pain at some point. You can't experience satisfaction in relationship without also experiencing dissatisfaction. You can only know one by comparing it to the other. For instance, you can't experience liberation unless you are also very familiar with confinement and constraint. To resist one side of any pair only postpones your embrace of the whole, and it is this embrace which is the purpose of our birth.

Intimate relationship, no matter how painful, provides us with a uniquely effective means by which to fulfill our purpose, to grow in love.

Wouldn't He Treat Me Differently If He Loved Me?

If he loved me, he would treat me differently. This is a dangerous assumption to bring to your intimate relationship. Men are often not sensitive to how they affect you. Try telling your man, "I feel unloved when you do this." Then work it out from there. But do not assume he knows he is hurting you.

If he turns away he is probably doing so because of his own need. Rather than assume he is rejecting you, assume he is needing love. Discover your own patterns, discover when you are withholding love, and when you are giving it. This is the real lesson to be learned in relationship.

You don't have to punish him back. If he turns away from you, you don't have to feel, "You turned away so I'm going to turn away." You can recognize his turning away as his own pain, his own call for love.

Realize that both of you will be opening and closing,

loving and turning away. This may continue for years. The relationship itself is your teacher. You can come to understand your own reflex mechanism of shutting down, of closing. Then, instead of feeling rejected or betrayed by your partner's unlove, you could help each other re-open in love. You can practice loving in relationship.

Expect that whoever you are with will hurt you, turn away from you and withhold their feelings occasionally. This is a normal part of a relationship because most of us have not yet transcended all of our patterns that are less than absolute love. We are only in the process of learning to be open. We are students in the school of love.

Why Should I Give Him Love When He Pulls Away from Me?

The cycle of coming closer together and then moving farther apart continues throughout a relationship. Even if you make some kind of formal commitment to get married or live together, this dynamic will continue. This dance will continue within the confines of the commitment.

The measure of a working relationship is not, "Can this dynamic stop?" This cycling between closeness and distance will probably continue. The measure of a working relationship is whether both of you can remain communicative during this dance. Can you remain open? Can you continue serving one another? Can you stay connected to your heart? Can you continue giving your gift of love, even when your partner hurts you by pulling away?

Observe your reactions to the ongoing dance of rejection

and desire. What do you do when he pulls away? Are you angry? Do you doubt yourself? Do you feel hurt? Do you hold yourself back until he does something? Do you give love no matter what he does? Observe your pattern in the dance of relationship. Are you practicing love or withholding it?

Rather than taking it as a personal insult, rather than needing his love in order for you to be loving, simply remain open as heart-feeling. You may be hurt. Your heart may be deeply wounded. However, it is possible to remain open even with a wounded heart.

When he pulls back you probably feel it as a rejection of you, but he is actually pulling back because of his own need. His withdrawal from you is an expression of his own need. You can practice love even when he pulls away from you. It is through your demonstration of love that he will learn love. It is through your vulnerable heart that his heart will learn to open and receive your gift of love.

When you feel rejected and pull away, you offer him nothing except distance. Closing your heart hurts him and you. Remain open and loving even when wounded by his turning away.

If you pull away when you feel rejected, then you are giving your man this message: "I will only love you when you show me love." What he hears is that love has to be earned. If you give this message to each other you will become performers, working to get love, instead of lovers, freely giving love to each other. Love is a free gift or it is not true love.

Why Should I Trust Him If He Hurts Me?

Trust is a matter of moment-to-moment practice. There will be moments of unlove that come between you and your man, but you can still trust each other's ability to practice love. When he turns away from you, you can still trust his process of practice; you can trust that he will recognize his turning away, breathe fully, connect with his true heart, and practice love. If you do not trust his ability to practice this recognition and return to love, then you are in a relationship that will only torture both of you.

On the other hand, your partner usually reflects your own patterns. If he is not able to recognize his closure and return to love, then you, too, are probably withdrawing and closing. For instance, if his closure hurts you and so you close down, then you merely reflect each other. If he becomes mechanical and unfeeling during sex and so you become angry and close your heart, then you merely reflect each other. You cannot oblige your partner to be more than an accurate reflection of you. You can only practice love, grow in your capacity to give love and trust love, and thus serve your partner's growth in love.

True intimacy requires active trust. If you are closed or turned away from him, you are in no position to serve his ability to love. But when you are present with him and trust in the process of love itself, then you provide him with a reminder of love. He will either respond in love, or he will not.

You cannot make him love. The best you can do is to *be* love. He will either meet you in love, or he will turn away. In either case, you are love. And your love will attract love, absolutely, either from him or from someone more capable of practicing love with you.

16

Embracing the Parents in Your Head and in Your Bed

Why Do I Always Get Involved with a Man Who Can't Give Me What I Want?

Most of the patterns that limit our intimate relationships develop in our childhood before we are two years old. They have no verbal components and no conscious mental components. They are emotional and physical patterns. Like digestion, they operate at an unconscious level even though they may be very complex.

If you look at the intimate relationships you have had, you will probably notice a pattern, a similarity. There are, of course, differences, but if you look at the similarity in each one, you may see the pattern of intimacy which started in your childhood.

Your emotional needs in an intimate relationship reflect the emotional needs you had with your parents. You want to be acknowledged as special, just like you did with your parents; you want to feel secure in your partner's love, just like you did with your parents; and you may want your partner to give you more attention, just like you did with your parents.

Very little of this is conscious. You don't see a man and say, "This relationship will match my childhood. I will try and get from my partner what I always wanted from my parents but never got." All of a sudden, we find ourselves recreating our childhood pattern once again.

As adults, we develop internal conflicts and stress because, although one part of us is unfulfilled by our intimate relationship, another part of us is actually satisfied by replicating our early childhood patterns. This is the part of us that is willing to settle for consolation and security. But there is a larger part of us that is not happy being stuck in a pattern which continually limits our sharing of love in relationship.

In our early childhood we learn, or take an imprint, from the "love" we experienced from our primary caretakers, usually our parents. The way our parents treated us, whether it was abusively or dotingly, becomes our template for love. It is like radar. When we are with a partner who treats us as our parents did, then our bodies and emotions feel: "Oh yes. This feels like home."

For instance, if one of your parents emotionally abused you, you will be unconsciously attracted to an emotionally abusive partner. If your father or mother neglected you, you will be unconsciously attracted to a man who won't provide you the attention you want. If your parents were critical of you, you will unconsciously be attracted to men who criticize you. You will unconsciously try to recreate the feeling of "home." No matter how unpleasant that situation was, your body still interprets it as "love."

In addition, people repeatedly try to get the love and acknowledgment from their intimate partner that they never got from their parents. They repeatedly engage the psycho-emotional dance they learned as children in rhythm with their parents, and attempt to lead that dance toward the feeling of love and acceptance.

For instance, if you were the "caretaker" of an alcoholic parent, you will tend to play the caretaker role with your intimate partner. If you got your parents' attention by being cute or even flirtatious, you will play the same role as "seductress" with the men in your adult life. If you learned to suppress yourself and agree with whatever your parents said, you will tend to do the same with your intimate partner.

It is inevitable. As children our emotional and even our physical survival depended on our parents' love. Our nervous system learned what it had to do to get it: smile, agree, perform, control, admit fault or act strong. As adults, we continue to unconsciously act out our search for love and acknowledgment in the form we learned as children with our intimate partner.

Remember, you will continue to unconsciously choose men who can't give you what you want, as long as you are trying to "get" love. You are actually *choosing* partners, unconsciously, who can't give you the love you want, in the same way your parents didn't give you the love you wanted. You will do this until you learn that you *are* the love you always wanted. Then you *do* love and open *as* love rather than seek it like a child.

How Does My Mother Affect My Intimate Relationship?

If you have an inner struggle because of an unresolved relationship with your mother, then you won't be able to fully relax into your feminine energy. And, it is only by relaxing into your feminine energy that you are able to open and receive your partner's masculine gift.

When you are no longer at war with your mother or any other aspect of your internal feminine energy, then you will be able to open and receive your man's gifts and also fully embrace him, gifting him as his source of feminine loving. If you can't completely relax in your own feminine, in your own body, then you won't be able to manifest your full love-radiance in reciprocal gifting with your man.

First learn to trust both masculine and feminine energies. Then, you can rest in your preferred energy and allow the other to become externalized in the form of your partner. By embracing him, you can enjoy the bliss of reunion between the masculine and feminine energies of love. Relaxing into your own natural sexual character, you can enjoy the exchange of masculine and feminine gifts, rather than arguing over issues of power, control, trust and emotional support.

Such arguments often arise because we reject some aspect of our parents, and therefore some aspect of our own sexual character. We no longer trust our own gifts, or the gifts of our partner. We are not completely relaxed in our body's desires. We do not trust that our partner will give us the love that we want. We do not trust our own sexual fullness, our own feminine or masculine gifts.

In order to relax in sexually polarized love with a man, you must be willing to relax in your feminine energy. Since your mother represents your deepest memory of the feminine, you must embrace her and accept her totally before you will be able to relax fully with your man.

You must embrace your mother to receive your man. Then your body, breath and sexual character will let go of any resistance to the full incarnation of your native feminine energy. If you are holding on to a conflict with your mother, you are holding on to a conflict with your own feminine expression of natural radiance.

How Can I Change His Need to Control Me?

One way to look at intimate relationships is to see them as an attempt to replicate our relationship with our parents, or the relationship we wished we had with our parents. Another way to see intimate relationships is as a vehicle for the practice of opening, growth and real love. We feel internal conflicts because both of these efforts are true of us: We are consciously trying to grow in intimacy, and unconsciously trying to replicate the often painful patterns of our childhood.

The way this conflict is resolved involves communication and learning to love *through* our limiting personality patterns. For instance, a man might have a need to be in control. Maybe when he controlled himself as a child, his parents rewarded him with love. Now, in his intimate relationships, he will automatically act controlling, because that's what feels like love in his body. Even though he may not be *getting* love for being controlling now, that's what his body demands. That's what feels like the door to love for him. He might be mystified because his relationships don't seem to work, but he will still do it.

For a man like this, it would help for you to communicate something like, "I am feeling hurt right now by what you are doing." It will be a revelation, because your man, at an unconscious level, will assume what he is doing will get him love, just like it did with his parents. But when you say to him, "I am being hurt," then it gives your partner a chance to realize his actions feel painful to you.

This way your relationship becomes a feedback device through which he begins to unlearn old behavior and associations. He will probably never completely unlearn them. The pattern is recorded deep in his body. But it doesn't have to be an obstruction to love. It could just be a humorous facet of the relationship. The way to dissolve the *force* of old patterns like this involves humorous communication between partners rather than blaming each other.

We have to be careful about condemning, blaming and

resenting our partner for having a painful pattern in intimacy. At some level, part of us may unconsciously desire this pattern; it is probably one our parents also had.

Just assume that when you enter a relationship, both you and your man will have patterns that need to be loved through. You can in effect, say to one another, "Let's love each other and let our relationship be a free arena in which to be amused by our hidden patterns."

By realizing that your man is not acting out his patterns toward *you*, then you are more free to smile and remind him of love. Don't expect his patterns to disappear. Rather, practice sharing love and humor even while the pattern arises. The pattern may *never* disappear, but you can learn to share love even now, whether or not the pattern arises.

Why Do I Feel Like I'm Still Trying to Please My Mother?

For all of us, "mother" is part of our psyche. We have internalized her. She is always going to be telling us what to do.

During childhood we internalize both of our parents. They punished us and rewarded us and we internalized this process. Now, we punish ourselves and reward ourselves in the same way. Any decisions we make about what we should do with our lives and relationships, and how to be safe and protect ourselves, are usually made by internal parental voices. Whether we feel good about ourselves or bad about ourselves, it is probably our internal parent who makes the judgment.

We often try to obey or resist our internal parents and become suppressed or confused by our own inner voices. Our inner parents tell us one thing, but our adult desire tells us something else. We are divided inside. As a child we listened to our parents and we still do, obeying and sometimes rebelling against our own internal voices. All of us, at times, find that one part of us wants to do something that another part of us thinks is bad or risky and unsafe.

You can say to your external and internal mother, "I know you are only trying to help and protect me. I am an adult now and sometimes I choose to rebel and take a risk. So, although I hear and appreciate you, I am choosing not to obey you. I am willing to learn from my own successes and failures in life."

If you have not made peace with your internal mother, then you will continually doubt your worthiness. It is time to realize that you do not have to do anything to become worthy of love! You deserve love exactly how you are, because you are made of love. Your nature is love. If you simply relax and allow your heart to melt through the tension in your body and emotions, you will express love. And if you express love you are lovable.

You do not have to please your mother. She's working through her own process. She is trying to fulfill (or has tried to fulfill) her life through you. She wants you to be the perfect daughter—*her* version of "perfect." You can choose to honor your mother's version of perfect, but it does not have to be your version. You do not have to oblige yourself to carry that weight. You are free. But to be free, you need to love your external mother as well as your internal mother. And when you love them you still don't have to behave for them. You don't have to be the "good" daughter.

Be who you are. Be all of you, sinner and saint, bum and workaholic. Embrace all the parts of you and love. This is your only true responsibility. It is a responsibility not because you are supposed to do it, but because *you are love*. To be love is the truest expression of who you are. Your mother may not accept you and you may not even accept yourself. You may suffer rejection from within, yet still *you* are love.

Your mother is learning her lessons in life. Let her go. Serve her in love and let her go. When your inner mother makes you behave "properly," simply smile and breathe through her. Love her. She is only the internal pattern of your external mother. They have both served you in your growth as a child, protecting you, teaching you and caring for you. But now you are ready to reclaim your life. You are ready for love. There is nobody, internal or external, that you need to be good for. You are free to learn by your own successes and failures. You are free to love and be loved, *exactly as you are*.

How Can I Get Rid of the "Mother" I Still Hear in My Head?

You may not like all of your inner voices, such as your inner mother. You may try to push some of them away. But the truth is, you have many voices inside of you. Some of them are pleasant, others are not. You have a saint inside of you as well as a sinner. You have a protective mother inside of you as well as a little baby who wants to be held and loved.

When you objectify all your internal voices, you understand and are aware that they are all part of the energy pattern you call "me." You also understand that your awareness transcends them all. The real you, the you that is always free and clear, is the you that is awareness itself. Growth involves greater and greater self-awareness. And the more conscious you become, the more you will have to face your inner cast of characters.

The characters we hate most in other people are the "characters" we hate most inside ourselves. If we hate lazy people, we hate the lazy part of ourselves. If we hate stupid people, we have developed an inner criticism of our own stupidity, perhaps from our parents reprimanding us as children. The way we have learned to respond to our internal cast of characters is also the way we respond to our external friends, family and enemies.

We don't have to obey any of the voices we hear, internally or externally. We can choose to push them away. But if we do, they will inevitably return. If we try to disown them and push them out of our lives, we are only strengthening their energy. For example, if we don't want to see the seductive part of ourselves, we will attract a display of seductiveness from others. We attract in others what we resist in ourselves.

The universe is moving toward greater and greater consciousness and love. The universe has its own divine intelligence. We are going to have to face our hidden parts, sooner or later, either within ourselves or in the guise of others. If we are unwilling to face the dark part in our own psyche, we will attract people into our lives who display the same darkness hidden within us. One way or another, we will be brought face to face with what we hate and fear most, so we can learn to love more fully.

In the end, you will learn that all the internal and external voices you hear are only part of a lifelong lesson of consciousness. You can try to please *others* by hiding parts of yourself. You can try to make *yourself* happy by hiding parts of yourself. Or, you can learn to be conscious of every part of yourself, including the parts you would rather not face.

Consciousness *is* freedom. You don't have to "get rid" of your inner mother to be free. To be fully conscious of all your parts, embracing them all instead of resisting them, is to be free. Even though you may hate or fear certain parts of yourself, they all developed for a reason in their own time, during your childhood.

No matter how conflicted you feel inside, remain fully conscious of all your inner motives, "good" and "bad." You *are* this force of consciousness. By choosing consciousness, you strengthen your true self, rather than getting lost in the inevitable conflict of inner voices that developed during your childhood, and that still blab on within you today.

17

Practical Exercises for Healing Your Relationship

What Can I Do When He Is in a Bad Mood?

The highest form of feminine radiance is love, which can be expressed in many ways. Men feed on this radiance. This love heals their hearts. When they receive it, men feel, *Yes! This is the woman I want to be with!* It is this radiance, this happiness, that shines through a man's bad mood.

Nothing makes a man happier than your happiness. Plan tonight this way: Be as happy as possible and give your happiness as much as possible. Give your happiness in the way you enjoy it, with energy and creative imagination. Don't imagine his negative reaction, *Oh, he'll never accept it.* Give him happiness the way you want to.

Kiss him, hug him, hold him, tell him you love him, tell him how good it is to see him. Do whatever expresses your happiness. He might scowl and mumble, "I don't feel like it. I feel horrible." Don't absorb his masculine refusal of life and energy. Transform the moment, literally, into a garden of life: music, loving affection, food and light. All of it is just an expression of your radiant happiness.

The feminine force is the force of life. Your happiness is the heart of this force. The masculine bad mood is all about dissociating from the force of life, but you don't have to withhold your gift just because your man tends to refuse you. The masculine always tries to avoid or manipulate the force of life. Take this into account, humorously, and be happy. Your feminine force of life is your unique gift to your man, and, deep down, it's what he wants from you, regardless of his resistance.

Men most readily receive their woman's happiness and energy in a physical way. That's why sex is often so important to a man: It's one way he feels love directly through the body.

Imagine that your man is in a typical, one-sided masculine orientation to life. *He feels, Life sucks. I've had a horrible day at work.* You can lift him out of this by offering him the gift of bodily life in the garden. Suddenly he tastes something incredibly delicious. He feels something warm on his skin. His muscles relax in your love. He drinks deeply of your energizing radiance.

It's the goddess coming to greet him which transforms his mood of "life is hell." This is the largest gift you could give him and yourself; to be connected with your own love and happiness, whether or not he is willing to receive you. If you are relaxed in, and giving, your native feminine energy, and he will not receive it month after month, then either you are with the wrong man or he is a very slow learner.

How Can I Tell Him I Don't Want to Be His Mother?

Your man probably treats you like mommy sometimes, and at other times he doesn't. Specifically, when you are sexual with him he probably treats you like a grown man treats his lover, not as a little boy treats his mother. If this is so, then in the moment you feel he is treating you like mommy, shift the energy by being sexual with him. Be overtly sexual with him, on the spot. If you don't want to go as far as sexual intercourse, at least touch him very sexually. This should instantly shift his energy from little boy energy to adult man energy.

It is good for him to be able to shift into his needy child energy now and then. But this energy could inhibit growth if it habitually pops up and prevents his full, masculine gift of love and integrity. The way to serve him is to help him feel the difference between his little boy energy and his adult man energy. You can demonstrate the difference by touching him sexually when he is in his little boy energy, instantly evoking his adult, masculine sexual energy. He will feel the difference and be able to grow and take responsibility for his own masculine energy.

Instead of telling him what he should be doing, which would depolarize him, just touch him like a woman touches her lover. He will probably respond by shifting into his adult man energy. As his recognition grows, he will be able to take more and more responsibility for his energy pattern in relationship with you. He will become aware of his tendency to trust you like mommy, and you will have a powerful yet humorous and sensual tool for helping him shift into his adult masculine energy.

How Can We Regain the Passion We Had Before We Became Parents?

Between children and work, many parents find themselves without much time for each other as lovers. If you can't arrange to have an hour together away from the kids, with at least some frequency, then you won't have the opportunity to relax as a lover with him. You will always be in your mother energy and he will be in his father energy. It isn't easy to relax into your lover energy with your children around.

As an experiment, try this for two weeks. Whatever it takes, arrange your lives so that for an hour every third day your children are out of the house and taken care of. You and your man are alone. It doesn't matter what time of the day or night it is. What does matter is that this hour is to be used for intimacy with your man.

It is important that your children are out of the house and well taken care of so that your attention is not compromised in any way by them. Furthermore, spend your hour together in complete silence. Do anything you want. Remain present together without leaving each other's company.

Practice this for two weeks and remember to remain silent. If you speak, you will probably fall into your old patterns again, talking about work, the children, your needs. The tone of your voice and your words carry the energy that defines your mood: tired mother, needy girl, good friend. If you don't speak, you are more likely to be simply present and open to intimacy. You will be feeling each other, simply and freely. You may touch or you may simply gaze into each other's eyes.

Just sitting in each other's company, silently and fully present, serves to move you into true intimacy. He may lean over and touch you or you may touch him. Allow for spontaneity. It will work out.

Allow time for his and your sexual energy to find their natural and relaxed expression. For this hour, you are not parents. You are lovers. His masculine and your feminine energy are dedicated to gifting each other with love, rather than to caring for your children. If you don't consciously make this time to be together in relaxed polarity, full-time parenthood will probably put an end to your sexual passion.

How Can I Learn to Enjoy Sex More?

Many women don't fully appreciate themselves as sensual beings. If you can't really enjoy your own body and take delight in all the sensations it can provide for you because of some form of guilt or shame, then you won't be able to fully enjoy sex with your intimate partner either.

In order to have a full sexual life with your intimate partner, learn to appreciate yourself physically. Take some time in private and give yourself permission to touch yourself everywhere, in any way that feels good. Don't necessarily touch yourself in order to achieve an orgasm. Touch yourself to relax deeply into the flowing energies of your own body, enjoying the force of your own pleasure. See if this doesn't open new possibilities of play with your intimate partner, or new ways you may consider playing in sexual love.

How Can I Stop Flip-Flopping Between Feeling Helpless and Feeling Strong?

Within you is a helpless part and a strong part. Within you is a part that thinks *I'm ugly* and a part that thinks *I'm beautiful*. There is a part that feels totally dependent on receiving love and a part that feels completely independent. Each of us has within us two sides to every judgment, mood and desire.

When you feel dependent on your partner, it means you are only listening to one side. When you feel independent, it means you are listening to the other side. When you have listened to one side for a long time, then it is healing to listen to the other side for a while. Wholeness is being able to witness and hear both sides within you, and to choose your action based on intuitive wisdom rather than on either of these voices.

To help you witness both sides within you, try saying out loud, "There is a helpless part of me and there is a strong part of me."

Or you can say, "I'm feeling confused and I also feel clear at times."

Whatever comes up in you—hurt or anger or wanting to be alone—acknowledge it completely, but don't acknowledge it as the only part. Instead, say something like, "I'm feeling the need to be alone, and at times I also feel the need to be with you." They are both true.

Here is another example: "Part of me wants to leave, but part of me wants to stay."

Both sides of a desire are always true. As you grow, you learn to accept both sides of yourself, and therefore both sides of your partner. You can even grow to accept, "I love you" and "I hate you." There are always two sides to every emotion.

Realizing that the whole includes both sides instantly relieves the moment of one-sidedness. Rather than feeling trapped, you are free to witness both sides of every desire, and choose your action from this place of clear awareness. Always say the whole. "I'm feeling happy now, and I also feel sad at times." "I'm feeling lonely now, and I have also felt loved." "I'm feeling angry now, and I have also felt compassion." "I don't want to be with him now and I do want to be with him at other times."

The practice of intimacy requires that we make free and clear choices. Such freedom and clarity arises when we embrace and witness both sides of every desire and emotion so we are no longer trapped by one side or the other.

How Can I Connect with My Intuitive Wisdom About My Relationship?

Sit quietly for a few minutes and center yourself. You can close your eyes or leave them open, whichever is more relaxing. Take several deep breaths and relax any tensions in your body or emotions.

Feel into the deepest part of yourself, deep into your heart rather than the words that are going on in your head. Rather than any particular emotional quality you may be feeling now, feel into your deepest self.

There is a fundamental undertone there, a constant sense of being. Allow yourself to feel into that most directly right now.

Visualize your intimate partner. If you don't have an intimate partner, visualize your potential or imaginary intimate partner. If you don't like to visualize, think about your partner, feel your partner or hear your partner's words. Contact your partner, or potential partner, through whatever way you can really sense him, through imagination, vision, touch, feeling, emotion or sound.

Feel what happens in your body as you imagine him or sense him. Is there tension? Do certain parts of your body open and certain parts close? Be sensitive to the texture of the different parts of your body as you hold the imagination of your partner approaching you and being with you.

What comes up in your mind? Are there thoughts about what he might do? If he wants you or likes you? Do you want him? Are there doubts? Just allow whatever happens to happen.

Allow your imagination or thought to continue, letting it go free form. Maybe you will begin arguing. Maybe you will begin making love. Maybe you will touch each other and talk. Find out what happens.

Then, from the very deepest part of you, your most knowing, intuitive place, allow a message to emerge to your consciousness. It can be a message telling you what to do, with respect to this actual or potential relationship, or perhaps a message that is a question about the relationship.

Allow your deepest self to communicate directly with your conscious, verbal mind about the relationship. Whatever spontaneously comes, let it come. And if nothing comes, that's fine.

Whatever spontaneously comes about the relationship, let it come.

Honor whatever part of you gave you that question or message. Do the same if no question or message was given. Honor the part of you that you call your partner, or your potential partner. Accept anything you felt or thought and release it, like the breath, inhaled and exhaled.

Open your eyes when you are ready. Practice relaxing and staying sensitive to the intuitive wisdom of your deep self, even when your eyes are open.

Is Discrimination or Surrender More Important for Real Commitment?

True commitment is to love. If your commitment is to another person instead of to love, then you will suffer. First of all, that person is going to die, sooner or later. And while alive, that person will change continually. So there really is no fixed or unchanging person that you can commit to forever, only the eternal love you share with that person.

The form of the relationship may change, too. Sometimes love is most increased by separation, temporary or long-term. By committing to love, you are not only being committed to the love in yourself but also the love in the other and the love that both of you bring into the world. You are committing to whatever serves the magnification of love.

The masculine aspect of love is the question, "What increases love—this option, or this option or this option?" The feminine aspect of love is trusting and opening, rather than weighing consequences and thereby guiding behavior. It is important that each of us exercise both our masculine and feminine aspects so that our intimate relationships are balanced.

The masculine aspect of intimacy involves the discrimination of what steps are best to take next to maximize the incarnation of love in our lives. The feminine aspect of intimacy involves a remembrance of love in the present; it is a relaxation, a surrender, into love now.

It is your gift as a feminine incarnation of the Divine to attract your man from his head into his heart and to invite him into love. It gives him tacit permission to feel, sexually as well as every other way, from his heart, rather than from just his head or his genitals. This gift is your embodiment of the feminine principle, of the goddess. The feminine is far superior sexually to the masculine. Gift your man with your superior energy and sensitivity and invite him into the realm of the feminine.

It is your gift to incarnate feminine love without fearful inhibition. You don't have to withdraw your energy, feeling, *He'd rather be working now so I shouldn't gift him.* You don't want to interfere with his path of truth, but there are many times when his path veers away from the truth of his heart into the needs of his head or genitals. In these moments, allow yourself to be free, to be wild and radiant in your unique way. Invite him into love, don't just accept where he wants to go. This is your gift to him as a woman, because the power of love is as inherent as your breath.

How Can I Clarify Whether I Really Want to Stay with My Man?

If you are trying to decide whether to stay with your present partner, you could use a daily contract as a tool. Every morning when you wake up you could sign a contract with your partner. It is either a marriage contract, a separation contract or a divorce contract. Every morning you select a contract for that day.

If you wake up and you feel divorced, you would sign a divorce contract for that day and live that day as if you were divorced. The next morning, you may feel married. So you sign a marriage contract for that day. Both of you then act as if you were married for that day. Each day is a new choice. Sometimes by shifting the energy and assuming, "Today we are divorced," the relationship is clarified. Relationship is not a given form. We often think that once we are married, that's that. But really, relationship is an ongoing decision.

18

Surrendering into Ecstasy

Can a Bad Relationship Prevent Me from Discovering God or Divine Love?

You don't have to go anywhere to discover God or Divine Love. The divine is inherent in this moment, in this place, wherever you are, now. Anytime you feel that another individual or a circumstance is somehow preventing your connection to God or Love, then you can be certain you are not being fully responsible for locating your connection to God or Love in the present moment.

Nothing and no one outside of you can prevent you from feeling God or Love in this moment. If you blame your intimate relationship for limiting your spiritual life, you are mistaken. You can refuse to feel Love, but it cannot be taken away from you by your partner.

Once we understand this, we can look clearly at ourselves. "What am I doing that is preventing me from feeling God or Love in my intimate relationship?" Then it becomes a workable situation. We are no longer acting as if it were another person's fault. We are actively taking responsibility for our moment to moment awareness of God or Love.

How Can I Experience Ecstasy in My Intimate Relationship?

When you take the word *ecstasy* apart into its root forms and look at what they mean, you find that the word literally means "to stand outside" yourself.

You are limited by the boundaries you assert in your daily interactions with others and the world. To be ecstatic is to allow your boundaries to dissolve so you are standing outside your usual, limited, sense of self. When your boundaries dissolve, you can relax into deep communion in love. This requires that you relax the actions which create your boundaries in the first place. Ecstasy requires you to surrender control. Communion with your partner in love requires that you feel through and beyond your limited sense of self.

Ecstatic love with an intimate partner requires feeling beyond your personal boundaries. If there is a part of you that resists giving up control, you will have difficulty releasing into ecstasy in your intimate relationship. If you think giving up control is somehow negative or weak, then you will not be able to surrender in ecstatic love with your man. To love means to trust. To love ecstatically means to trust so deeply that you allow your boundaries to melt in the force of love.

The intimate man-woman relationship involves two equals, of course, but man and woman are not equivalent. That is, the feeling of being a woman in love and the feeling of being a man in love are very different bodily feelings. Being a woman in love involves feeling your body open in more and more complete trust.

Trust doesn't mean being foolish. It doesn't mean doing something stupid. Remain intelligent in your trust. However, trust does require letting go of control with your intimate partner and abandoning yourself in love. Then the force of love is magnified by the natural energy of sexual polarity and you are released from your limited sense of self into the bliss of ecstatic communion in love, a love that has no boundaries.

How Can I Love Without Getting Hurt?

The boundaries that obstruct you from ecstasy are put in place by your ego to protect you from hurt. In fact, your ego *is* the process of forming these boundaries. Surrendering yourself beyond these boundaries necessarily involves surrendering yourself to the possibility of being hurt. This is the nature of vulnerability or openness in love. It involves facing your biggest fears, and relaxing through them.

Love, or love-ecstasy, requires vulnerability. You are required to be open to the possibility of being hurt. If you want love, if you want ecstasy, you must submit yourself to the possibility of being hurt. Eventually, you must let down all of your guards and trust that love will always result in growth, whether the process is temporarily painful or pleasurable.

This doesn't mean you blindly surrender yourself completely to the first man who walks by. Maintain your intelligence about it. Try your best to pick a man who is also committed to this practice of mutual vulnerability and growth through love. Once you have found such a man, your practice is to actively love. This means letting down your guard, feeling through your fear, and remaining open at the heart, connected with your partner. Allow yourself to be hurt in love. Allow love to wash through the hurt.

If you actively practice love but your man consistently refuses to practice with you, then you should move on. You haven't lost anything. You have strengthened your ability to remain open, relax in vulnerability and practice active love. The practice of open-hearted vulnerability will develop in you a radiant and forceful disposition of love that helps attract the kind of man who is ready to practice at your level. He will be as willing as you are to let down his guard, even though he is afraid; open his heart, even though he may be hurt; and actively love, even though it feels like a risk.

Should I Just Passively Surrender to Whatever My Man Wants to Do?

The only form of surrender which is worth doing is surrendering to love—not to another person, to your own ideas, or to the way things are now going. True surrender does not mean to just go along with things and remain passive. True surrender is to surrender to love and then to allow love to express itself with full force and freedom.

The wise way to surrender is to feel love as much as you can in the present moment, surrender into that loving and then energetically bring this love forth in your life and intimacy. Surrender doesn't mean you say to yourself, "He's doing something I don't like and I'm getting angry. I'll just surrender and go along with it." This isn't surrender. It's passivity. It's suppression.

True surrender is the ability to feel your essence, to feel your love, and surrender everything that prohibits this love from shining. In doing so, you let go *as* love. You are radiant as this love. You let love live *as* unobstructed force and feeling. This is true surrender.

Do I Have to Surrender Myself to Really Enjoy Sex?

Most people, at one time or another, have experienced something close to perfect sex. Moments of complete passion—heart, body and mind totally abandoned in love. Some people have gotten fleeting glimpses of sex like this. Others have felt this way for years. And still others have only dreamt of it.

Whether you have experienced it or not, can you imagine what it would be for you to be completely abandoned in sexual passion? In that moment, you and your man are abandoned in ecstasy. You are both surrendered in love.

When you are surrendered, you are not weak, but wild. In ecstatic love-embrace, you are completely open and surrendered and he is completely open and surrendered. He has let go of all inhibitions and has submitted and abandoned himself in love. He has abandoned himself beyond the sense of self, and you have, too. Your man is penetrating your heart and body with love. The more lovingly he enters your depths, the more you open. Your openness invites him further in ecstatic loving. His loving enters you, and your heart widens for more.

The feeling of being ecstatically abandoned in the sexual loving of your man is the feeling of being ravished in love. His forceful, sensitive, masculine love pervades your open body and heart.

His loving may be strong or passionate, but it's not cruelly violent. Your loving may be wild or receptive, but it's not craven or passive. Whether vigorous or serene, in ecstatic sexual communion your boundaries are loosed, your hearts are expanded, and you are both surrendered into the radiant force of love.

Am I Ready to Surrender into Love with a Man?

You have probably experienced letting yourself go and surrendering yourself at some time or another. You might have abandoned yourself in sexual passion. You might have looked at your child in a moment of complete love and felt no boundaries. In those moments you lose your separative sense of self. You look into your lover's eyes, or your child's eyes, and suddenly you are aware of the One who is love, not two separate people.

This feeling of oneness occurs when you sacrifice your boundaries and allow yourself to be continuous with the one you love. You let go of your guard and relax into surrendered union, experiencing the ecstasy of seamless joy.

When you are making love, for instance, you can either hold on to yourself or let go. If you are holding on, you feel self-conscious while you are having sex. Ecstasy, however, is when you let go of your borders and allow yourself to love without limits. When you let go of yourself in love, such a moment is ecstatic. You lose your sense of self in the heart widening bliss of love.

Learn to cultivate this blissful sacrifice of self as a practice, moment to moment. Practice letting go of the sense of your self-definition, your sense of "me," your feeling that, *I am here and these are my boundaries. Don't cross them.*

However, there is a prerequisite to stable relaxation in this ecstasy: In order to let go of your boundaries you must first develop a strong sense of boundary. To sacrifice your sense of self, you must first develop a strong sense of self. Without first developing a strong will, you won't be able to relax through the fear that arises when you explode in the ecstasy of love and completely let go. As your identity merges into the force of love, you will fear you are becoming dependent on a relationship or are losing something you are not ready to relinquish.

You can't go directly from being needy and weak-willed to being free in ecstatic surrender. First, you have to let go of your dependency on others and develop a strong sense of center, a strong sense of self. Your inner divisions must come to an essential harmony so that your sense of center is unified. You must be made single in your intent. Your will must become strong. Then, and only then, are you prepared to sacrifice yourself directly into love.

For More Information

To order books or audiotapes by David Deida, call 24 hours a day:

Toll-free 1-888-626-9662

(or call 1-813-824-7972 for information)

BOOKS by David Deida

Intimate Communion
Awakening Your Sexual Essence

It's a Guy Thing
An Owner's Manual for Women

The Way of the Superior Man
A Man's Guide to Mastering the Challenges of Women, Work and Sexual Desires

The Way of the Superior Lover
A Spiritual Guide to Deep Sexual Bliss

AUDIOTAPES by David Deida

Intimacy to Ecstasy
An Interview with David Deida

The Shiva and Shakti Scales
Our Search for Love and Freedom

Kinks, Consciousness and the Plumber
Talks on the Embodiment of Spiritual Practice in Love and Intimacy

For more information about David Deida's books and workshops or to schedule a presentation contact:

David Deida Seminars
6822 22nd Ave. North #142-G
St. Petersburg, FL 33710
Telephone: (813) 824-7972
Email: info@cyberplexus.com